Early Acclaim
for The Practice of Awakening II
The First Light of Joy

"The true purpose of our existence here on Earth is to have Joy, and then once achieved, to help others achieve it. **Paul's Practice of Awakening II is a pathway to that Joy which is rightfully ours.** He has written it as only a master can do, for it not only shows us the way but also gives us the tools to ensure we stay on the path. Paul has the uncanny ability to ignite the light within us and discover that the answers to living a life of Peace, Happiness, and Joy are within us all"

~ Roger Anthony, International Speaker, Author and Founder of Crocodiles International

"Great wisdom most often comes in the form of simple unadulterated truth. In each of the beautiful poems and clear messages in The Practice of Awakening II, Paul Hoyt shares **intimate insights from his journey of Awakening. His life lessons are everyone's life lessons.** I plan on adopting them to my life NOW."

~ David M. Corbin, Author, Illuminate: Harnessing The Positive Power of Negative Thinking, Wylie and Sons, 2012

"As I read Paul's book, I felt like a Spiritual Voyeur, peaking into the heart, soul and mind of an angel-human. **His writings are both examples and reminders of great truths. His vulnerability and humility serve as a way-shower for others who aspire to live an awakened life.**"

~ Eve Hogan, speaker and author of The EROS Equation: The Soul-ution to the Relationship Problem

"It has been a real joy watching Paul grow in Spirit and Consciousness these past few years. And now you can see his journey unfold, too, as **he shares the lessons of his lifetime with us, in simple words that we can all understand.** The Practice of Awakening II is quite a beautiful spiritual journal!

~ Nick Berar, The Soul Whisper

"Paul's beautifully expressed personal journey **lights the way for others on the path of self discovery and enlightenment.** It is a beautiful roadmap for the seeker!"

~ J. Karen Frank, Founder, A Crystalline Light Foundation

The Practice of Awakening II imparts **profound and practical inspiration for the spiritual path.** Paul Hoyt hits a high note!

~ Elaine M. Christine, Ph.D., author, The Peace Prophecy: Vision 2013

"The Practice of Awakening II" is **a valuable compilation of brief simple lessons designed to draw your own inner wisdom out of you.** That's a daily practice we all can benefit from. It reminds me of the old classic Notes to Myself by Hugh Prather."

~ Dr. David Gruder, Bringing the Wisdom of Psychology to Business, the Wisdom of Entrepreneurship to Helping Pros & the Wisdom of Both to Social Change

"Why not learn from someone on the path? Paul shares deeply what he has learned and what he still needs to aspire to. **He does not have "the answer" or simple pablum… he just tells his truth of his Awakening as it unfolded. Thanks Paul, for the openness and vulnerability** in peeling back your onion. You have served up a rich spiritual meal for those on their own path."

~ Stewart Levine, Resolutionary, author of "Getting to Resolution," "The Book of Agreement," Collaboration 2.0" and the forthcoming "Pilgrim's Path: A Morning Practice."

"In his usual way, **Paul speaks candidly, deeply, and thoughtfully** from the 'I' perspective of his personal, professional and spiritual journey, and somehow subtlety ends up speaking to the hearts and minds of all of us. A quick, insightful and awakening read!"

~ Keith Wayne MacGregor

"Paul's new book, "The Practice of Awakening II" is **a reminder for me to let go of fear, disappointment, and anger to see what takes its place.** I was feeling fear this morning and recognized an urge to give in to the fear's energy to run away.

I had Paul's "The Sixth Gremlin" open on my desktop and read it at that moment. I was reminded to slow down and relax, enabling me to redirect the energy that the fear was providing into a useful purpose.

Thank you Paul, for giving us these reminders to be reunited under the guidance of a higher power!"

~ Robert Mertens, Artist

"We have an amazing ability to be changed by the experience of another's story. In The Practice of Awakening II, Paul Hoyt weaves **inspired writing with bits of humor, nudges of coaching, and divine guidance, from his soul's journey.** His unveiled thoughts and reflections come through these pages, inviting you to listen lovingly to your own deep yearnings, and to find innate wisdom all your own."

~ Tambra Harck, Founder and Spiritual Director, Emergent Women

"Authentic self expression at it's best. Paul's words, or 'Simple Truths' always give me a new perspective and act as a catalyst for me to explore another level of Spirituality."

~ Bill Heinrich, Author, The Seven Levels of Truth

"The journey to our inner light has so many layers to it! And Paul's style touches them all with the elegance and grace of his open heart – opening the deepest corners of our truth – letting those simple truths be revealed. **Very inspiring writing that touches so deeply."**

~ Les Jensen, Writer, speaker and Founder of New Human Living

"Awareness of what is – is the first step to really living, fully within, with a depth of 'awakening' to the reality of what moves us. If we are to be self-actualizing human beings, 'being' in this world, then it is essential to truly become in tune and stay in tuned with what moves and resonates with our essence. Paul Hoyt's collection of poems, missives, and expressions in The Practice Awakening II can help you journey back to what you connect with in your life. **Simple truths, beautifully expressed for your awareness to your own 'Awakening'."**

~ Sue Lee, CEO of EQ Media, Inc. and Creator of award winning program "I Believe in Me!"

"How can we find deep inspiration and evolution in every moment of our lives? Paul Hoyt's intriguing collection of insights in **The Practice of Awakening II enables us to have more joy, peace and awareness of our true loving selves, by inspiring the wisdom within us**."

~ Jason Nelson, Bestselling Author of Empower Our Children: God's Call to Parents, How to Heal Yourself and Your Children

"Finding a way to breathe without re-afflicting our soul's choice by the echoed fears of our past requires 'the practice'. The practice of Self Awakening in Paul Hoyt's latest book **will assist those intending to re-awaken the genius within.**

~ John Pearson, Founder, First Source Institute

How do you awaken more fully to your joy, peace and inner wisdom? The Practice of Awakening II gives **meaningful lessons in bite-size segments that are the light of simple truths.** Allow Paul Hoyt's journey to enrich yours with practical ways to apply awakening principles to support you in embracing your own sacred Self."

~ Linda Radford, Clarity Catalyst, author of Intuitive Vital Keys Mini-Course

Paul Hoyt has such an amazing spirit, loving nature, and insatiable thirst for knowing. His beautiful reminder of the importance of "Saying No" in a way that honors all involved is very powerful. Each insight in The Practice of Awakening II provides multi-layered comprehension of the intricate tapestry of our existence. **What an amazing gift he's given the world!**

~ Tonya Dawn Recla, Personal Power Expert

In this book Paul Hoyt describes in an authentic and engaging way, the journey that we all take regardless of our present levels of success or fulfillment, as we try to make sense of the ups and downs of each chapter of our life. **His humble and down to earth communication style** with which he generously shares his wisdom, insights and inspiration earned by living life consciously and with purpose, is valuable and accessible to people from all walks of life. **Paul's messages convey higher levels of awareness and consciousness that are available to all of us if we are willing to keep moving forward** through the valleys and summits as he has done. His wittings contain many blessings and shine a light on many of the shadows, obstacles and paths that we all must travel as we strive to become the person that we know we can be.

~ Berel Michael Weiner, Emotional Intelligence and Communication Coach

Creating our dream business and life requires that we master the inner game. Paul Hoyt's insights in The Practice of Awakening II helps you do that. **Read it, apply it and see the results.**

~ Annette Bau, founder MillionaireSeries.com, author of The 7 Principles of Becoming a Millionaire for Life

Also by Paul Hoyt

Inspirational Works

The Practice of Awakening – 150 Ways to Raise Your Consciousness Whenever You Choose (2010)

Remember – A Simple, Gentle, Powerful Pathway to Your Magnificent Potential (2005)

Business Works

Beyond Business Survival – The Key to Thriving in Business (2013)

The Capital Coaching Program (2010)

The Foundation Factor – Critical Measurements of Business Strength (2004)

The
Practice
of
Awakening II

The First Light of Joy

Paul Hoyt

Copyright © 2009-2012 by Paul M Hoyt.

Cover design / illustration by Heart Centered Media

Angel Star illustration by Robert Mertens.

Published by Paul Hoyt & Associates, LLC, Santa Clara, California, 95054. (www.paulhoyt.com)

All rights reserved. No part of this book may be used or reproduced by any means, graphic, electronic, or mechanical, including photocopying, recording, taping or by any information storage retrieval system without the written permission of the publisher except in the case of brief quotations embodied in critical articles and reviews.

This book is dedicated to all of my teachers.
I am grateful for the lessons they helped me learn.

Table of Contents

Foreword and Acknowledgements 1

Always Becoming 5

Everybody Is 7

One More Time 9

Seriously 11

The Sixth Gremlin 13

The Balcony 15

Idle Circuits 16

Amazement 18

Small Paul 19

Levitation 20

A Six Step Path 21

Delighted, Excited, and Feisty! 22

Freedom 23

The Law of Polarization 25

Sometimes 26

Always 28

Stepping Up 29

Touching 100 Lives 30

My Dearest Team of Angels 32

Any Virtue Will Do 34

Nourishing Waters 35

We Are 37

Spiritual Food 38

Affirmations 39

Understanding	40
Joyfully Creating	42
Reminders	44
I See It	46
No Power Over Me	47
Transcending the Path	49
Interaction	50
Nothing in the Way	52
Dealing and Healing	54
The Swimming Pool and the Eye-Dropper	56
Pure Heart	58
Once More, With Feeling	59
Saying No	61
The Many Ways of Letting Go	62
Shining Brightly	63
100 Voices	65
The Vital Energies	67
Not Going There	70
Independence	71
Always Sending Love	73
My Blind Spot	74
On Stage	75
Vibrational Variability	76
This Moment Too	77
Resistance	80
The Great Turning	81
The First Light of Joy	83

Excitement!	85
Barking Dogs	86
The Right Path	87
Even Though	89
Wonderful and Amazing	91
I Will Not	93
Perspectives on Transforming	94
Watching Triads	95
This Time	97
Even Though II	99
Beyond Transcendence	100
Thousands of Times	101
I've Been Here Before	103
Checking In	105
Fear	107
Vision Star	109
The Dawning of Consciousness	110
The Choice	112
My Voices	115
Thank You Spirit	116
The Flip	119
Becoming	120
The Blessings of Humility	121
Action and Adventure	123
Joy Walking II	124
Fireflies	125
I Am	126

An Eight Step Path 128
The New Remember 130
The Responses 135
In The Light 138
Healing Tears 139
Magic Storeroom 141
60 144
Variations on a Theme 145
Energy Shivers 147
The Dreamer-Creator 148
I Forgive Myself 149
Do Unto Others 151
Humility II 153
Staying Awake 155
Being Awake 157
Energetic Momentum 159
Anxieties 160
Feeling, Thinking, and Requesting 163
Flavors of Bliss 164
The Icing or the Cake? 166
The Amazing Bliss of Beingness 168
Sherry's Book 169
Bliss List I 171
Bliss List II 174
Empowering, Relaxing, and Awakening 176
Blessed Beyond Measure 178
The Fear of Life 180

I Do	182
Tree Hugging	184
Imagining My Life	186
The Gush	187
Just the Right Thing	188
The Other Side of Fear	190
Hurry!	191
Purposeful Breathing	192
Base Camp	194
Five Choices	195
Buzzes, Zings, Fogs, and Lamps	197
The New Deal	198
The New Assessment	199
Celebration!	201
New Rules	202
Necessary and Sufficient	204
Six Foundational Paths	206
The Baseline	208
Moments	210
The Depths of My Conditioning	212
The Cake is Done	214
The ABC's of Enlightenment	216
No	218
Surrender	219
Watching From the Stillness	221
It Takes a Lot of Strength	223
The Wisdom Factory	224

Morning Prayer	225
Life is a Celebration!	226
Some Will Think II	227
The Lineup	228
Something in Store	230
The Choice II	232
After	234
The Most Beautiful Things	236
Instead	238
Overconfidence	240
Nature Therapy	242
The Problem is Not the Problem	243
Watching, Watching	245
Outer and Inner	247
Ethereal	249
The Many Ways	250
Easy	251
The Journey	253
Today's Focus	255
Before	256
Yes	258
Even Though III	260
Always II	261
No Sacrifice	262
Attachments	264
Life	266
Stronger and Safer	268

Fear Ladder 270
Mahara 271
Maharami 273
About the Author 275

Alphabetical Table of Contents

100 Voices	65
60	144
A Six Step Path	21
Action and Adventure	123
Affirmations	39
After	234
Always Becoming	5
Always II	261
Always Sending Love	73
Always	28
Amazement	18
An Eight Step Path	128
Anxieties	160
Any Virtue Will Do	34
Attachments	264
Barking Dogs	86
Base Camp	194
Becoming	120
Before	256
Being Awake	157
Beyond Transcendence	100
Blessed Beyond Measure	178
Bliss List I	171
Bliss List II	174
Buzzes, Zings, Fogs, and Lamps	197

Celebration!	201
Checking In	105
Dealing and Healing	54
Delighted, Excited, and Feisty!	22
Do Unto Others	151
Easy	251
Empowering, Relaxing, and Awakening	176
Energetic Momentum	159
Energy Shivers	147
Ethereal	249
Even Though II	99
Even Though III	260
Even Though	89
Everybody Is	7
Excitement!	85
Fear Ladder	270
Fear	107
Feeling, Thinking, and Requesting	163
Fireflies	125
Five Choices	195
Flavors of Bliss	164
Freedom	23
Healing Tears	139
Humility II	153
Hurry!	191
I Am	126
I Do	182

I Forgive Myself 149
I See It 46
I Will Not 93
I've Been Here Before 103
Idle Circuits 16
Imagining My Life 186
In The Light 138
Independence 71
Instead 238
Interaction 50
It Takes a Lot of Strength 223
Joy Walking II 124
Joyfully Creating 42
Just the Right Thing 188
Levitation 20
Life is a Celebration! 226
Life 266
Magic Storeroom 141
Mahara 271
Maharami 273
Moments 210
Morning Prayer 225
My Blind Spot 74
My Dearest Team of Angels 32
My Voices 115
Nature Therapy 242
Necessary and Sufficient 204

New Rules 202
No Power Over Me 47
No Sacrifice 262
No 218
Not Going There 70
Nothing in the Way 52
Nourishing Waters 35
On Stage 75
Once More, With Feeling 59
One More Time 9
Outer and Inner 247
Overconfidence 240
Perspectives on Transforming 94
Pure Heart 58
Purposeful Breathing 192
Reminders 44
Resistance 80
Saying No 61
Seriously 11
Sherry's Book 169
Shining Brightly 63
Six Foundational Paths 206
Small Paul 19
Some Will Think II 227
Something in Store 230
Sometimes 26
Spiritual Food 38

Staying Awake 155
Stepping Up 29
Stronger and Safer 268
Surrender 219
Thank You Spirit 116
The ABC's of Enlightenment 216
The Amazing Bliss of Beingness 168
The Balcony 15
The Baseline 208
The Blessings of Humility 121
The Cake is Done 214
The Choice 112
The Choice II 232
The Dawning of Consciousness 110
The Depths of My Conditioning 212
The Dreamer-Creator 148
The Fear of Life 180
The First Light of Joy 83
The Flip 119
The Great Turning 81
The Gush 187
The Icing or the Cake? 166
The Journey 253
The Law of Polarization 25
The Lineup 228
The Many Ways of Letting Go 62
The Many Ways 250

The Most Beautiful Things	236
The New Assessment	199
The New Deal	198
The New Remember	130
The Other Side of Fear	190
The Problem is Not the Problem	243
The Responses	135
The Right Path	87
The Sixth Gremlin	13
The Swimming Pool and the Eye-Dropper	56
The Vital Energies	67
The Wisdom Factory	224
This Moment Too	77
This Time	97
Thousands of Times	101
Today's Focus	255
Touching 100 Lives	30
Transcending the Path	49
Tree Hugging	184
Understanding	40
Variations on a Theme	145
Vibrational Variability	76
Vision Star	109
Watching From the Stillness	221
Watching Triads	95
Watching, Watching	245
We Are	37

Wonderful and Amazing 91
Yes 258

Foreword and Acknowledgements

Evolution is defined as "The gradual development of something."

Such is the story of my life. I have gradually become a much different person than I was a decade ago, experiencing life in a much different way, attracting and manifesting much different things.

My evolution from caterpillar to butterfly took the better part of a lifetime.

There was no real tipping point. I wanted there to be one, of course, praying and pleading many times to have an immediate and permanent transformation into The Angel Within, but it never happened.

Instead, it happened gradually, one Awakening at a time.

My evolution continues. My thoughts, feelings, and perspectives continue to be fine tuned.

I seem to be walking The Path of a Thousand Lessons. Lessons like how my subconscious mind was formed and how I can change it. Lessons about the power we each have to transform ourselves into persons of greater Love, Peace, Wisdom, Power, and Joy. Dozens of step-by-step paths to Return to Spirit.

And as I learned and relearned the lessons of a lifetime, I wrote them down. I recorded them so I could remember and relearn them, and so I could share them with you.

This book is the sequel to *The Practice of Awakening – 150 Ways to Raise Your Consciousness Whenever You Choose*, published in 2010. Unlike that book, this time I am sharing the messages in the same sequence in which they were learned.

It has helped me to review them in that way, and I can see my consciousness evolve over the three-year period in which they were written.

And that is my wish for you – that I can support you in your evolution, help you learn your lessons and put pieces of your life-puzzle in place in ways that accelerate your transformation into the person you want to be, so that you experience life in the way you want to experience it.

I do.

Now, I do.

I have had a lot of help along the way. I am deeply grateful for the guidance from my immediate family, who top my list of supporters. Thank you Sherry, Steve, Curtis, and Alyson.

Over the last eight years, I have also worked with 28 spiritual teachers and coaches in some way, including Roger Anthony, Nick Berar, Elaine Christine, Karen Frank, Ram Giri, Jaya Gopal Das, Tambra Harck, Bill Heinrich, Andrea Hess, Eve Hogan, Les Jensen, Lori Kochevar, Sue Lee, Stewart Levine, Keith Wayne MacGregor, Aliah Majon, Robert Mertens, John Morris, Jim Mulvaney, Jason Nelson, John Pearson, Suzy Prudden, Linda Radford, Tonya Recla, Don Saunders, Monique Schoneau, Marsha Valutis, and Berel Weiner. I probably left someone off the list, so please know that you contributed to my growth, too.

In addition, my favorite speakers, authors, and bloggers include Bob Proctor, Esther Hicks, David Corbin, Byron Katie, Mary Morrissey, Eckhart Tolle, Rhonda Britten, David Gruder, and Esperanza Universal. I have also read countless small articles, inspirational quotes, and messages.

My Facebook home page is full of the lessons of my lifetime. I have had thousands and thousands of conversations with others about this Journey of Life.

It is my wish to become one of those inspirational voices in your life, as so many others have been in mine.

Namaste.

I encourage you to take this book with you, so you can quickly and easily read one or more messages when you have a few minutes to spare. Put it in your briefcase or purse, so you can Practice Awakening whenever you choose.

Always Becoming

I have noticed some resistance lately in taking the next steps in my evolution. Not always, of course, but some of the time. I have this deep desire, it seems, for my Journey to end – I want to reach that Safe Place where I have Become, and am no longer at risk of slipping back into the darkness. I want to reach that place where I am *always* Blissful and Conscious.

Today in my morning meditation I focused on the Energy that is constantly moving through me and how I am Always Becoming something, as the Energy shifts within me and around me throughout the day. I respond to internal and external stimuli, and I change. At any given point in time, I have Become what and who I am, and at the same time, I am Always Becoming something new.

But what am I Becoming? Am I allowing whatever comes my way to change me as it will, or am I choosing to move upwards? Am I paddling or floating on the ever-changing currents of Energy?

My choice is to make my "Always Becoming" my "Always Awakening". I choose to always be choosing and to Awaken with every shift of attention.

I choose to be Always Becoming The Angel Within.

Do you see how you are Always Becoming? Do you notice when you are trending up or trending down? What are you allowing and what are you choosing to be?

Suggested Exercise: Step back and watch yourself change throughout the day. Be diligent in your Self-Assessment and Courageously Honest about what you see. In some way large or small, choose to become the person you want to be.

Everybody Is

Self-Awareness continues to become more and more fine-tuned. I spend a lot of time in Silence observing the workings of my subconscious mind. Checking in and releasing is a most interesting game with a magnificent payoff!

And as I continue to check-in with myself throughout the day, I notice that I am sometimes a little bit stressed, a little bit afraid, a little bit angry, a little bit unconscious, or maybe a little bit crazy. Sometimes all of the above, and sometimes more than others.

While I experience an ever-increasing quantity of Peace, Joy, Strength, Wisdom, and Love in my life, there are still some of these other experiences, too. There is still work to be done: to Remember, Embrace, and Become my Higher Self. Moment by Moment.

And as I look at others, it appears to me that the same is true for them: like me, they are a little bit stressed, a little bit afraid, a little bit angry, a little bit unconscious, or a little bit crazy. Sometimes all of the above, and sometimes more than others.

Everybody is.

Do you see times in your day when you are a little bit stressed, afraid, angry, unconscious, or even a little crazy? Do you see the same in others? Do you see the Love and Light in Yourself? Do you see the Love and the Light in them, too?

Suggested Exercise: Make some notes today of the times you notice you are being less than your Higher Self. And when you notice the challenges that others are experiencing, Practice Humility.

One More Time

I have been gaining in Humility gradually and steadily over the past several years. Yesterday, I became even more humble.

As Proud, Encouraged, and Blessed as I am to come into The Spirit, to Remember and Return several times every day, it occurred to me that I forget as much as I Remember.

If I am in that Blessed State of Grace, it is because I have Remembered one more time than I have forgotten. I remembered that The Spirit is but a thought away.

If I find that I am not in a State of Grace and that there is some work to do, then I have forgotten one more time than I have Remembered. I forgot the power that I have to choose to live In The Spirit.

One more time.

After 30,000 times or more of Remembering and Returning, I am Humbled that I still have not permanently learned this lesson. I am still developing the Habit of Higher Consciousness.

For now, I continue to forget and Remember, forget and Remember, over and over again, every day.

And Right Now, I choose to Remember.

One more time.

How often do you Remember the Power you have to choose to be In The Spirit? Once a year? Once a month? Several times a day?

Suggested Exercise: Keep count of the number of times you Remember and Return today. Reflect on the perspective that you have forgotten only one time less than you have Remembered, and talk to a friend about it.

Seriously

In the practice of Unconditional Joy, I am finding times where I am tempted to be Serious, usually because someone else is serious. But seriousness implies some sort of worry or fear, as in "we need to have a serious conversation", or someone is "in serious condition", or "I am taking myself too seriously".

With seriousness, there is an implication of the potential of pain or disaster – seriousness often means something is wrong or potentially very wrong, and the word carries that negative energy for me.

But I find that fear is only helpful to the extent that it triggers me to focus on a significant situation. Once I am focused, fear is not my best partner: Peace, Joy, Strength, Wisdom, and Love are my best partners. I prefer to live in a State of Grace, and fear is not a part of it.

So while I understand that many people are "serious" (i.e., "worried") a lot of the time, I choose to be Quietly Joyful, Focused, Sincere, and Respectful instead.

I choose a Lightness of Being.

I choose this State of Grace.

Otherwise, my Joy is conditional and limited.

Seriously. ☺

Are you serious much of the time? Is that just a nicer way of saying that you are worried or afraid? When you come into a serious situation or talk to a serious person, are you aware of the fear behind the seriousness?

Suggested Exercise: Practice Unconditional Joy for a few hours today. Note the fears and worries you let go of as you do. And no seriousness!

The Sixth Gremlin

Yesterday was a bit of a down day. There was some low-level tension that I couldn't quite shake. There was a "disturbance in the force".

Today, I went through my Path of Songs in the morning and came back into Spirit and a marvelous State of Grace very quickly, after I found my Sixth Gremlin.

As a reminder, my other five gremlins are Fear, Forgetfulness, Complacency, Attachment, and Unconsciousness – when I am not at my best, one or more of these almost always names the problem. I wrote about them in The Practice of Awakening.

But this time, it was different. This time, there was a Sixth Gremlin, a subtle variation on Fear that was a combination of a Sense of Unworthiness and a Fear of Rejection. Deep in the foundations of my Soul, these wounds were bubbling up. Unworthiness is my sixth gremlin.

Someone had been especially critical of me, and it triggered me to experience my deepest shadows. The fear was exposed. It took me awhile to remember that I really was a Worthy person.

In a way, it is nice to be working at that level. Now that the fear and pain is gone, I can more easily reflect and learn the lesson.

And I know that when I heal that wound, I will have taken a great step towards being One With Spirit even more frequently and powerfully than I currently am.

Do you ever experience a sense of unworthiness? Do you have, at some level, a fear of rejection? What lesson is the pain teaching you today?

Suggested Exercise: Look at your fears and your pain as lessons, as opportunities to heal yourself and Grow in Spirit.

The Balcony

In a dream last night, I saw the world from the balcony of a theatre.

Once again I had become the Spirit Who Used to Think He Was Me.

I was surrounded by other Spirits who used to think they were human, too, looking down at their avatars on the stage of life.

The actors were projections of the Spirits sitting beside me – and there I was, too, on the stage playing my role. Learning, growing, acting.

We were all chuckling a bit, because the actors thought they were real!

How freakin' hilarious is that?

Do you think you are human? Have you ever considered that you might be just a dream of Spirit instead?

Suggested Exercise: Visualize yourself in a balcony with all your Spirit friends watching The Play of Life unfold before you.

Idle Circuits

There are these Idle Circuits in my subconscious, waiting to be triggered by some external event or internal focus. When the stimulus occurs, a small, barely noticeable buzz might sound, a tiny little light might shine, or a huge explosion may erupt.

Some of them are Happy Circuits, some are not. When I hear a baby laugh, a Happy Circuit is always triggered. When I walk peacefully in nature, a Happy Circuit is always triggered.

When someone spews negative energy my way, my Defensive Circuits are triggered to some extent. Sometimes I just buzz in response for a second or two; other times the response is much louder and longer lasting. I used to live in the Pit of Darkness nearly all the time when my own internal negative thoughts almost continually triggered the Defensive Circuits. Explosions, internal and external, were frequent and expected.

My practice these days is to be in a State of Grace so that the Happy Circuits are easily and quickly activated, and such that the Defensive Circuits are defused.

Being my Loving Presence and my Joyful Spirit does that.

Being The Angel Within day after day is increasing the number, size, and, strength of the Happy Circuits. Living in a State of Grace reduces the number, size, and strength of the Defensive Circuits. Being a Peaceful, Silent Watcher blankets the Defensive Circuits such that they are diminished.

Or turned off completely.

What external events have triggered your Happy Circuits and your Defensive Circuits today? Which thoughts have you had that triggered them?

Suggested Exercise: Choose several thoughts or experiences today that trigger your Happy Circuits. Find a lot of them. Make a list.

Amazement

I woke up this morning with an incredible sense of Amazement. Everything about life seemed more Amazing than ever – my body, my thoughts, my feelings; the fan, the bed, the ceiling; each breath, every heartbeat, etc.

I was Energized at the opportunity to experience these things and Energized to be aware of my experiencing.

The Amazement was followed by a chuckling-out-loud Joyfulness and a deep sense of Gratitude.

The perspective continues as I go about my work, talking to clients and exploring partnerships. I wonder how long it will last today.

I have written several times about how Amazing life is to me, and how everything seems so Beautiful, Amazing, and Precious when I am in the Sacred Flow of Life, when I am living in a State of Grace.

Today, for some reason, that perspective is so powerful that it brings Tears of Joy to my eyes.

Amazing!

Do you ever just Marvel in Amazement at this Experience of Life? When was the last time you did so?

Suggested Exercise: Make a list of the top 10 Amazing things about life. Refer to it three or more times today. Cultivate your sense of Amazement.

Small Paul

There seem to be three different self-images in my Awareness today: Small Paul, Angel Paul, and Spirit Paul.

Small Paul is the person who is a little sad, discouraged, lethargic, angry and stressed. When he realizes that he is being small, he almost immediately remembers the Angel Paul – that aspect of who I am / who he is that is Peaceful, Joyful, Strong, Wise, and Loving – the Angel Within.

Then there is the Spirit Paul, or more accurately, the Spirit who Used to Think He Was Paul, sitting in the balcony, watching his avatar-self vary in Consciousness, watching him move between being Small Paul and Angel Paul.

Beyond the Joy and Suffering.

Watching.

Do you have three or more dramatically different manifestations of your life? How often are you the Small version, the Angel version, and the Spirit Version?

Suggested Exercise: Practice these perspectives today. Become the Angel version and the Spirit version of yourself several times.

Levitation

I was talking to one of my coaches yesterday expressing some frustrations around the interactions in a small group I regularly attend. Not much progress was being made. The stories and the challenges seem to be remarkably the same month after month.

He suggested that although I had learned to levitate, I had not learned how to teach others to levitate.

How true!

My Practice of Awakening is to become The Angel Within and live in a State of Grace every day, many times each day. It is a glorious personal accomplishment for me.

Teaching others to recognize the opportunity they have to do the same thing is the next step. Becoming an effective Spiritual Teacher, Mentor, Coach, Guide, Facilitator, Director is next on my list to learn.

Holding that space, being a role model and providing an example of the value of personal and spiritual development is my new goal.

And by helping others Learn to Levitate, I know I will float a little higher off the ground, a little more often, myself.

Are you teaching other people what you know about Spiritual Growth? Are you being a shining example for them? Right now?

Suggested Exercise: Make a point to be an example for others today. Be encouraging and supportive. Be at your best and help them make progress on their Journey.

A Six Step Path

Here is a new, very effective Six Step Path to Spirit or any other goal I have:

- I want / desire / need
- I can / I believe
- I will / I choose
- I act / I do
- I become / I make progress / I am productive
- I am / I achieve / I accomplish.

There are 216 variations in these simple choices (3*2*2*2*3*3), so I think it is highly likely that there are one or two that will work for me any time I choose. ☺

What variations of the Six Step Path appeal to you right now? Which words resonate with your Subconscious?

Suggested Exercise: Determine your favorite variation, your own personal path and practice walking it today.

Delighted, Excited, and Feisty!

As this new passion for helping others begins to develop, this new pride in reaching out and doing what I can to facilitate personal and spiritual growth begins to blossom, I find that I have a renewed energy and enthusiasm.

I am Delighted, Excited, and Feisty!

I haven't felt Feisty in a long time. But suddenly, I feel eager to challenge others, to engage them in debate, to get their attention, and to wake them up a bit.

I feel like playfully kicking someone in the butt.

I am Delighted and Excited to try out my new, shiny, pointy-toed boots on someone's backside, and I am not the least bit afraid of the outcome.

Watch Out!

When was the last time you felt a little Feisty and totally unafraid of a debate or confrontation? What would it take for you to feel that way again?

Suggested Exercise: Engage in a playful debate today.

Freedom

A few days ago, I woke up with the most wonderful sense of Freedom. For years I have consciously and subconsciously wanted to be a great Business Consultant, great Singer, great Public Speaker, and recognized Spiritual Teacher.

At some low level, my self-image and self-worth was dependent on achieving those goals. I worked for decades to feel in my own mind that I had accomplished those goals and had become "that person".

And now that I am there, I have a marvelous sense of Freedom to do other things.

Instead of needing / wanting to be a Business Consultant, I could be a real estate investor, C-level officer at one company, or run a string of car washes.

Instead of needing / wanting to be a great Singer or Teacher, I am OK with not being in the spotlight or behind a microphone. It's still fun of course, but not necessary.

Instead of needing / wanting to be a great Spiritual Teacher, I am content to live quietly in a State of Grace, sharing My Experience and My Truth with others as seems appropriate.

I feel like I just graduated from college and am ready to do and be whatever the Universe presents to me.

How exciting!

Are you free to be someone new? Or are you on a mission and "need" to be or do something specific?

Suggested Exercise: Be honest with yourself about what drives your self-image and self-worth. Discuss it with a friend who can also be honest with themselves.

The Law of Polarization

The Law of Polarization is simply this: when you tap into your power more greatly, when you "amp up" your energy, you increase your magnetic field enormously. That shift in your magnetic field has a strong impact on the people you encounter.

Fundamentally, you will attract some people and repel others much more than you did previously. You will not get as many lukewarm responses, and you make it more difficult for people to ignore you.

Some people who used to be attracted to you or who found you very comfortable to be around will suddenly be repulsed. You will scare them.

Others who would not have been attracted to you at all will suddenly find you irresistible.

That is both the Price You Pay and the Blessing You Receive by increasing your energy, your assertions, and your expressions.

And it is worth it.

Have you been shrinking away from your own Truth in fear of the responses of others? Are you prepared to be polarizing?

Suggested Exercise: Try speaking up a little louder and being a little more assertive than usual. Watch for those who are repulsed and those who are enamored.

Sometimes

I met him in college, but I don't remember his name. I think he was only there one year.

He was slender, but with wide shoulders. He had long hair and a full beard. He looked like Jesus.

The women were drawn to his Joyful Exuberance. He was very cool. I was very jealous.

I commented on how much I admired his charm, his strength, and his way with the ladies, and told him in some way how cool he was, and his response surprised me.

He simply smiled and said "Sometimes".

Not only was he cool in so many ways, he was also detached and observing his own moods, much like I do today. He was noticing his ups and downs, and the times he was stronger than others. He was not caught up in the moment.

I think he was the first person I ever met who had that talent, who had the Power of Detachment. In that second of sharing his perspective with me, I think something was triggered deep in my Soul – an Awareness, perhaps, of the possibility of a different State of Being.

And now, after years of work and countless hours of introspection, I spend most of each day in a State of Grace, where detachment is a cornerstone of my experience.

And my "Sometimes" has become my "Most of the Time".

And some days, it is Nearly All of the Time.

Do you experience a State of Grace Rarely, Sometimes, or Most of the Time? What are you willing to do to come to the point where you stay there Nearly All of the Time?

Suggested Exercises: 1) Ask yourself "Am I there?" several times today. 2) Keep a log of the times this week you experience a Blessed State of Grace.

Always

I always have some Level of Consciousness, from Totally Unconscious to Completely Awakened.

I always have some sort of an Attitude, from being Angry or Depressed to being Joyful and Loving.

I always have some sort of a Perspective, from being totally focused on the moment, to be Detached and Watching this moment from the context of my lifetime.

The question is: "What Level of Consciousness, what Attitude, and what Perspective am I experiencing right now?"

And the bonus question is: "Why am I choosing to experience this instead of something else?"

Hmmm….

Are you able to step back and discover the Level of Consciousness, Attitude, and Perspective you are experiencing Right Now? How often during the day do you do that?

Suggested Exercise: Stop right now and write down what you are feeling, thinking, doing, and experiencing. Take a step back and assess yourself several times today.

Stepping Up

This morning I woke up with an increased sense of Clarity and Determination – a realization of the Power that I had to choose to be at My Best. I found myself saying over and over:

> *I choose to be as Peaceful as I have ever been.*
>
> *I choose to be as Joyful as I have ever been.*
>
> *I choose to be as Powerful as I have ever been.*
>
> *I choose to be as Wise as I have ever been.*
>
> *I choose to be as Loving as I have ever been.*
>
> *Right Now!*

And once again, I see that I have been settling for less. I have been OK with feeling a little meek, a little weak, and a little embarrassed. My productivity and enthusiasm has not been as high as it could be and will be.

And so I am Stepping Up.

Stepping Up to the next level of who I Already Am.

Have you ever had a moment like this, when you suddenly realized the power you had to Step Up?

Suggested Exercise: Try Stepping Up Right Now! Choose to be at your best! Come on – do it!

Touching 100 Lives

For the longest time, I wanted to be famous and well respected, to be on the stage with luminaries and to be thought of as a Wise Man and a Great Spiritual Teacher.

But as I continue to make progress on my Journey, the desire to be acknowledged by the masses is fading away.

I simply don't care much anymore.

As I grow in Confidence and Humility, I find that my desire for fame has been replaced by a deep passion to help as I can. Just to share My Experiences and My Truth in such a way that I can touch the lives of a few people.

So I have a new mission: to Touch 100 Lives – to make a big difference in the lives of a few. To help them make progress on their journey, to help them with a little understanding and a little encouragement.

Maybe it will be a poem or a reflection, maybe it will be a hug or a smile, but in some way large or small, I am committed to being a Light in their Life.

I want them to know that I Really Do Care and that I Really Do Love them!

100 Lives. That is all.

And when that is done, I'll Touch 100 More.

Forever.

How many lives have you touched today? Are you spreading Sunshine, or spreading something else?

Suggested Exercise: Keep a silent list of the times you shared your Wisdom, Joy, Love, Strength, and Peace with another person. Make it a goal to Touch 100 Lives, and then Touch 100 More.

My Dearest Team of Angels

My Dearest Team of Angels,
Hear me Right Now,
    as I Ask and Allow
For Goodness to Flow into my Life.
With Ease and Grace,
    bringing Smiles to my Face
And so it is Done, and I Thank You.

My Dearest Team of Angels,
I am Grateful for the Goodness that is now Flowing into my Life
    and I Thank You.
It is Flowing with Ease and Grace
    bringing Smiles to my face
And so it is Done, and I Thank You.

My Dearest Team of Angels
I am grateful for the Goodness that has Come into my Life.
    and I Thank You.
It came with Ease and Grace
    bringing Smiles to my face
And so it was Done, and I Thank You.

Do you pray to the Angels? Do you believe that you have your own Team of Angels just waiting to serve you in some way?

Suggested Exercise: Practice this little prayer a few times. May it bring great peace to your soul.

Any Virtue Will Do

The nice thing about the Path of Remembering is that I can focus on any Virtue of the Spirit and return to the Spirit.

I can focus on Peace, Joy, Strength, Wisdom, and Love individually or in combination.

I can focus on Abundance, Health, and Power.

I can focus on Gratitude, Forgiveness, Self-Love, Detachment, Humility, Guidance, Patience, Compassion, Amazement, Oneness, or Openness.

Or I can simply sit in Silent Awareness.

Perfect Focus, Perfect Alignment, Perfect Resonance with any of the Virtues elevates me to Spirit,

> and then I am filled with all of the other virtues, too.

It is the most Amazing thing!

I just Choose,

> Focus,

>> and Return.

Do you practice the Path of Focus? What virtues or combination of virtues works best for you?

Suggested Exercise: Focus on The Angel Star – Peace, Joy, Strength, Wisdom, and Love – today to the exclusion of all else, until you Return to Spirit.

Nourishing Waters

I Float in the River of Peace.

>I imagine a magnificent river, miles wide and flowing gently to the sea. I am floating in the middle, completely silent and relaxed, moving slowly to the Ocean of Love. I am Nourished, Rested, and Healed.

I Play in the Fountain of Joy.

>I imagine a huge fountain in a bustling city square, having dozens of statues with water pouring out and spraying into the air in all directions. There are dozens of children playing with me there, squealing with delight. I jump into the water and splash around with them. What Fun!

I Stand in the Waterfall of Power.

>I stand powerfully at the base of a tremendous waterfall. There are millions of gallons of water pouring over me. The sound and the energy are astounding! The water empowers me as it protects me and flows through me. I Can Accomplish Anything!

I Drink from the Cup of Courage and Confidence.

>I lift the Cup of Courage and Confidence to my lips and drink the warm, nourishing liquid. It immediately radiates through my entire body and I am Energized, Empowered, and Triggered into Action.

I Draw from the Well of Wisdom.

>There is an ancient bucket in my hands, filled with water from the Well of Wisdom. As I drink deeply, I am filled with Clarity and Insight – I am

a Sage again. The Wisdom of the Angels is with me and I am Silent.

I Live in the Ocean of Love.

I am a water creature, swimming deep in an Ocean of Love. The Love is all around me for miles in every direction. I breathe Love, move in Love, and communicate with Love. I am Love.

Do you resonate with the Nourishing Waters? Which one works for you best Right Now?

Suggested Exercise: Practice this meditation a few times today.

We Are

Over the years, I have invested much time in focusing on the concept of "I Am".

I Am Spirit having a Human Experience,

> I Am One with God,
>> I Am my Higher Self,
>>> and so on.

A few days ago, as I was having an "I Am" Moment, I became aware of something new – a profound feeling that it was only a phase, a perspective to pass through.

And that the next perspective was the great "We Are".

We Are Spirits having a Human Experience.

> *We Are* One with God.
>> *We Are* our Higher Selves.

We Are the Same – unique in our own ways, but the Same.

We Are One not only with God, but with Each Other.

We Are Becoming.

We Are Alive

We Are.

Do you have a sense of the great I Am? Do you have a sense for the great We Are?

Suggested Exercise: Practice Embracing the Oneness today. Meditate on the great We Are.

Spiritual Food

I was a bit hungry the other day and I thought to myself "this is a small problem, easily solved with a protein bar, a piece of fruit, or a drink of water. The next meal is only a couple of hours away. I'll be fine."

I was a bit discouraged shortly thereafter, and it occurred to me that my Spiritual Body was in need of nourishment, much in the same way as my physical body was.

I knew the discouragement was only temporary and easy solved with some Spiritual Food. I knew it would only take a little poem, a sweet song, or a stretch to ease the stress a bit. I knew it would only be a couple of hours until I had my next Spiritual Meal in the form of a deep meditation or long walk, and there were dozens of things I could do to Nourish myself in the meantime.

So I sang a little song, gave a little thanks, and was filled with the Beauty of the Spirit once again.

I didn't have to wait at all. There was plenty of Spiritual Food at my fingertips.

Do you have a little Spiritual Hunger? Are you feeling a little discouraged or angry? What can you do right now to feed your Soul?

Suggested Exercise: The next time you notice that you have a little Spiritual Hunger, make a point to have a little Spiritual snack. Feed your Soul. The food is all around you.

Affirmations

I am Accepted.

I am Respected.

I am Admired.

I am Encouraged.

I am Worthy.

I am Forgiven.

I am Embraced.

I am Protected.

I am Guided.

I am Loved.

I am Free.

(repeat)

> *How do you feel about these affirmations? Do they ring true to you right now?*
>
> *Suggested Exercise: Say this over and over a few dozen times. Allow the process to be Uplifting and Connecting.*

Understanding

For the umpteenth time in my life, I was Healed a bit more through the Power of Understanding yesterday. A Spiritual Coach asked a great question, and I remembered events from long ago that were most likely the cause of some residual Fear and Unworthiness.

I Understood my Feelings. My blocks made Sense, and I was no longer afraid, ashamed, or embarrassed. In my Understanding, I was Liberated and Free to Move On.

My Understanding facilitated My Healing.

I am not sure why that is. I suspect that I am a Reasoning Machine, and I am troubled when feelings don't make sense. I am frightened when I am confused. When I see a rational, plausible reason for my feelings and my blocks, then I can simply let go of them.

I realize I don't have to feel the way I feel. There was an event or series of events that caused my Faulty Programming.

Theoretically, I could just let go of the blocks without knowing the reason for their existence, but I do not always choose to do that. It's easier when I Understand.

I don't think it makes any difference whether the reason is "true", but rather, it only matters that it makes sense to me and I believe it.

It is the belief in the Reason
       that evokes the Understanding
              that facilitates the Release.

Do you have a strong Need to Know? Have you had times in the past few days when some insight was very comforting?

Suggested Exercise: Note how the Path of Understanding impacts your life. Write down your insights you can refer to them and share them.

Joyfully Creating

One of my favorite Spiritual Teachers, Andrea Hess, cautioned her blog audience the other day about using the word "effortlessly" when setting intentions. Progress in this dimension requires action and effort – not struggle, but work.

Her advice: focus on Joyfully Creating your future instead of wishing for it to manifest with no effort.

So I created this little song to focus my energy:

> *I am Joyfully Creating my Day!*
> *I am Joyfully Creating my Day!*
> *Love, Peace, and Prosperity are Mine in Every Way*
> *When I'm Joyfully Creating my Day!*

> *I am Joyfully Creating my Life!*
> *Yes, I'm Joyfully Creating my Life!*
> *Only Peace and Happiness – the end to fear and strife*
> *When I'm Joyfully Creating my Life.*

> *I am Joyfully Creating Right Now!*
> *Yes, I'm Joyfully Creating Right Now!*
> *When I sing this silly song, my Spirit Soars and How*
> *And I'm Joyfully Creating, not just Anticipating,*
> *I'm Joyfully Creating Right Now!*

Do you believe that you have to struggle to succeed? Do you believe that Intentions and Prayers alone will manifest in this dimension, or do you see the importance of Action and Effort?

Suggested Exercise: Memorize all or part of this song, and repeat it whenever you are a little too serious.

Reminders

I was challenged by my coach yesterday to realize that I was still full of crap. He reminded me that as long as I had subconscious or conscious resentments, anger, judgments, disappointments, or other forms of negative energy of any kind, that there was still some work to do.

I loved it! I felt strangely eager to pursue the darkness that remained deep in my soul.

And a couple of times during the day, I noticed the negative energy well up inside, triggered by a little aggression from a colleague, and by a call from a previous client who owed me money. I responded with Patience and Kindness, but the negative energy was definitely there. I was clearly judging them, criticizing them internally in some way. It sure wasn't Unconditional Love I was feeling!

And this morning as I woke up in meditation, I learned a Fine Lesson.

I saw my resentment, anger, doubt, fear, discouragement, criticism, blaming, shaming, judging, and all other forms of negative energy as Reminders:

>Reminders of the Pain and Beauty of the Human Experience.

>Reminders of the Work I have Done and the Work that Remains.

>Reminders to be Patient, Kind, and Confident.

>Reminders of the Power I have to Choose to Love.

And I set my Intention to let each one of them serve as a trigger to Love Myself and to Love Others.

>Deeply and Completely.

Then, for the next two hours, I let every breath and every heartbeat be a stimulus to Love.

Love, Love, Love, Love, Love
> Over and Over Again
>> Every Second
>>> for Hours.

And when I arose, the Bliss continued.

Is there still some work to do? Are you working on resolving the lightening bolts of negative energy that are triggered throughout the day, or are you working on little jolts and buzzes?

Suggested Exercise: Write down a list of the ways you are (still) full of crap.

I See It

I see what Abraham sees.

I see what Eckhart Tolle sees.

I see what Byron Katie sees.

I see what Jesus sees.

I see what Buddha sees.

Not quite as clearly.

Not quite as consistently.

But in some measure, and some of the time,
> more Frequently and Deeper over time
>> I See It.

I See It.

I Definitely See It.

Do you See it too? What do you See? If you were to See it too, what is it that you would See?

Suggested Exercise: Make a list of the ways you are like Jesus and Buddha. Work on expanding the list.

No Power Over Me

I just realized that all of the people who trigger negative energy with me

    Those who have treated me unfairly

    Those who kicked me off the team

    Those who have been critical of me

    Those who owe me money

        Have No Power Over Me.

They cannot limit my Success.

And that goes for all the people I haven't met –

    Who might treat me unfairly

    Who might kick me off the team

    Who might be critical of me

    Who might refuse to pay me –

        They Have No Power Over Me, either.

They cannot limit my Success.

They only serve to Remind Me of My Power.

Who do you think is standing between you and your success? Are they really limiting you? Really? How can you be incredibly successful in spite of their imagined interference?

Suggested Exercise: Imagine that the people you think are limiting your success are only in your life to remind you how powerful you are. What would you do if that were true?

Transcending the Path

When you get close to the top of the mountain,
> You Transcend Your Path.

You see that it is but one of a thousand paths.

You see that growth is not about the path,
> it is about the destination.

And the more attached you are to your Path,
> The less likely it is that you will be able to Transcend It
>> And Reach the Top.

Are you still attached to your path? Are you proud to be a Christian, Muslim, Jew, or Buddhist – are you attached to your path – or are you grateful to be Embraced by Spirit?

Suggested Exercise: Practice letting go of your path. Surround yourself with Beautiful People who are walking different paths.

Interaction

The time has come for Interaction.

For all of the Angels, Archangels and Spirit Guides waiting for some Signal to Interact with me in some Grand Way, here it is:

- **For those Waiting for my Command,** I hereby direct you and command you to come into my Present and 1) Heal this silly sense of unworthiness that remains, and 2) Make Yourself Known to Me.

- **For those Waiting to be Set Free,** I am unshackling your chains forever – so that you may now rush into my Present and 1) Heal this remaining sense of unworthiness, and 2) Make Yourself Known to Me.

- **For those Waiting to be Asked,** then hear my passionate request: please come into my Present and 1) Heal this remaining sense of unworthiness, and 2) Make Yourself Known to Me.

- **For those Waiting for Permission,** then hear my decree: I hereby open up the doors to my conscious and subconscious mind and allow you to come into my Present – you have My Permission – to 1) Heal this remaining sense of unworthiness, and 2) Make Yourself Known to Me.

- **For those Waiting for Me to Let Go,** you who would Embrace me, Take Me Over, and Become Me, I now Surrender, Let Go, and Release all resistance. The time has come for you to come into my Present and 1) Heal this remaining sense of unworthiness, and 2) Make Yourself Known to Me.

That should about cover it.

And if there is anything else I need to do in order to receive these blessings and Interact with You, please let me know.

Until I hear from You, I will assume that I have done everything that needs to be done, and trust that you are on your way.

And I will carry on, Joyfully!

Are you walking and talking with the Angels? What do you think you need to do in order to Interact?

Suggested Exercise: Say this little prayer every day for a week and see what happens!

Nothing in the Way

As I continue to heal this deep wound in my soul, this Fear of Rejection and this Sense of Unworthiness, I am inspired to embrace some very useful concepts.

While I may be rejected from time to time by some people,

    I know I will never be rejected by Wise and Loving people,

        and I know that I will never be rejected by God.

Unconditional Love, God's Love, comes to us as do the Sunshine, the Wind, and the Rain.

    The Sun shines on every rock in the garden.

    The Wind moves every tree

    The Rain nourishes every flower.

They do not ask anything of the rocks, trees and flowers.

    There is no concept of worthiness,

        There is nothing to forgive,

            There is nothing to prove.

Man, in his silliness, may build structures that prevent these things from occurring in nature.

But unlike the Rocks and Trees and Flowers

    We have the power to move out of the shadows

        Out of our mental prisons

            Back into the Light, the Wind, and the Rain.

There is nothing to earn, nothing to forgive, nothing to prove.

There is nothing in our way.

> *Do you think that God's Love is somehow withdrawn from some people? Or is it that they have mistakenly gone into a cave?*
>
> *Suggested Exercise: Meditate on how God's Love is for everyone and over all time, like the Sunshine, the Breezes, and the Rain.*

Dealing and Healing

I continue to experience some Negative Energy in my life – little buzzes of impatience, hesitation, resistance, fear, anger, insecurity, discouragement, etc.

When those moments come up, I analyze, categorize, organize, and document them. I search for the triggers that brought them to life, and I search for the events in my life that caused those triggers to form in the first place.

I rarely ignore them – I deal with them.

And when I am finished with my mental gymnastics, I move on.

I focus on Positive Energy.

I shift my posture, I let go of my stress, I quiet my mind, I sing a little song, I repeat a mantra, or I recite a little poem.

I Remember the Power I Have to Embrace and Become The Angel Within, and then I do it –

> I Embrace It and I Become It.

I Forgive Myself.

I Love Myself.

I take Courageous Positive Actions in the Face of my Fear.

I become a Playful, Joyful, and Productive Person again.

And by doing so, I Heal Myself.

Dealing and Healing.

Dealing and Healing.

Hour after hour, day after day.

Forever, so far.

How do you deal with the negative energy in your life? Do you ignore it? Is it so strong that it takes considerable energy just to hang on? How do you deal with it?

Suggested Exercise: Make a list of your favorite ways to heal yourself; then, when the negative energy arises, Practice Awakening.

The Swimming Pool and the Eye-Dropper

I was talking to a dear friend the other night when she related the story of yet another man who went to bed one person, and woke up quite another.

He said it was like Someone New had come down and taken over his body. He was Born Again, all at once, and perhaps permanently. I expect that he became a person of great Peace, Joy, Strength, Wisdom, and Love, like so many others before him. All at once.

But such has not been my Journey.

I am Becoming, to be sure, but not all at once.

My Journey has been more like filling up a Swimming Pool with an Eye-Dropper. One drop at a time.

> With every Meditation, Prayer, Song, Reflection, or Reading.

> With every Act of Kindness, Patience, Forgiveness, Acceptance, and Love.

> Drop by Drop, the Pool has been filled.

To be sure, there have been times where I have been able to throw in a bucket or two of Divine Spirit in the Pool,

> and some days it seems like I am filling it up a cup at a time,

>> but there have been and still are a lot of individual drops deposited.

For me, the very good news is that the Pool is nearly full.

And I am now Blessed Beyond Measure.

How much water is in your Pool of Divinity? How quickly are you filling it up?

Suggested Exercise: Take a break from the filling and enjoy swimming for a while. Then help someone fill up their pool.

Pure Heart

In a meditation last night, I became aware that I had come to a place where I had a Pure Heart.

No resentments, no regrets, no anger, no criticisms, no desires, no needs, no despair, no fear – no negative energy of any kind.

Just a Pure Heart,
>filled with Pure Love
>>for everyone and everything.

And so I wrote this little song this morning:

>*Pure Heart, Pure Love*
>
>*Pure Heart, Pure Love*
>
>*Joy Abounding*
>
>*Strength Resounding*
>
>*Peace Astounding*
>
>*Angels Surrounding*
>
>*My Pure Heart with Pure Love*

Join me sometime, and I'll sing it for you.

How Pure is your Heart right now? Have you ever experienced having one? Do you remember what it feels like?

Suggested Exercise: Remember or imagine what it feels like to have a Pure Heart and Unconditional Love. Feel it as deeply as you can.

Once More, With Feeling

These days, I often find myself repeating a series of directives to my subconscious mind. Simple, one word commands such as:

> Come!
> Yes!
> Now!
> More!
> Spirit!
> Again!

Each one has a deeper meaning to me that is triggered by the single word:

- **Come!** reminds me of my frequent requests for the Angels and the Angel Within to come into my Present, to Connect, Protect, Guide, and Love me, and for my Decision to Come to Them.

- **Yes!** reminds me of my commitment to Becoming, to Surrendering and Transforming. It expresses my Willingness, my Intention to Evolve.

- **Now!** reminds me that the Only Time We Have, and the Only Time for an Awakening, is Right Now.

- **More!** reminds me not be complacent, but rather to continue Opening, Receiving, and Growing.

- **Spirit!** reminds me of the Angel Within, and the beautiful Spirit that is my Higher Self.

- **Again!** reminds me of my process of Remembering, Embracing and Returning to this marvelous Spirit within.

The sequence of the words doesn't make a difference. In practice, I find that mixing them up is more effective than repeating the same pattern over and over. So I might say:

- Yes, Spirit, Come, Again, More, Now!
- Now, Again, Spirit, Come, More, Yes!
- Spirit, Now, More, Yes, Come, Again!

Some of the variations start to make sense as sentences, and others do not. Each is effective.

*So **Now**, I return **Again**. I say **Yes** to the wonderful **Spirit** Within, and experience **More** Love and Light in my life. I have **Come** once again to a communion with the Angels, who have once **Again**, **Come** to me.*

Do have any simple one-word reminders that you can give to yourself? Do you understand how to develop them?

Suggested Exercise: Focus on developing our own list of one-word reminders and directives. Practice using it every day for a while.

Saying No

There are a lot of ways to say "No" from a place of Strength, Wisdom, and Love, for example:

When I disagree:
- "I don't see it that way"
- "I have a different perspective"
- "That's not the way I see it"
- "That's not my experience"

When I don't want to do something:
- "I am not open to that"
- "That's not a fit"
- "I'm going to go in a different direction"
- "That's not my first choice"
- "I don't want to do that"

I add a little "Hmmm…" to the start or a "right now" to the end when I want to soften the message, for example:
- "Hmmm… I'm not open to that right now" or
- "Hmmm… that's not the way I see it right now".

Hmmm….

How do you say "no"? When are you harsh and judgmental? When are you gentle and compassionate?

Suggested Exercise: Practice saying "no" a lot today, in ways that are Authentic and Gentle.

The Many Ways of Letting Go

There are so many ways of Letting Go:

- **I Let Go and Back Off** when I am frightened; I am still wary and observant and not completely detached.
- **I Let Go and Relax** when I am less fearful, and I can watch the situation while feeling safe.
- **I Let Go and Surrender** when I am totally open to what comes next, with not even a hint of resistance.
- **I Let Go and Leave** when I feel comfortable leaving the attachment behind.
- **I Let Go and Refocus** when it is time to hold a different perspective or do something else.
- **I Let Go and Forgive** myself and others, completely. I hold no resentments, grudges, or regrets.
- **I Let Go and Love** when there is some healing to do, and I come to a place where I can see the Gift and the Blessing in the attachment, and I am ready to Love Myself.

I think I will practice Letting Go today.

How many ways do you have of Letting Go? Are you practicing them every day? Are some easier for you than others?

Suggested Exercise: Make note of the times and the ways you Let Go today.

Shining Brightly

I was watching American Idol last night, when one of the contestants expressed a bit of fear during a performance.

One of the judges said (paraphrased): "Your job isn't to worry about whether the person in the third row likes you; your job is to feel as deeply and sing as passionately as you can".

On the same day, I watched a video from Ron Heagy where he related a story about being ill, and wondering whether he could make it to and through a speech at a school. He did, and young men and women told him of how his choice to carry on gave them inspiration to carry on, too.

I also watched a video about a lady in Texas who was a master at sewing quilts, and had made over 500 of them – even though she was completely blind. A number of years ago, she asked God to show her a way to be useful, and she found it.

And here I am, with this amazing talent, this incredible Love and Passion to help others, these beautiful messages and songs, still a little nervous and worried about how the person in the third row will receive my messages – still a little concerned over whether they will like me.

It is a humbling perspective.

Clearly, it is time to channel more Love, Joy, and Power.

Clearly, it is time for me to Shine More Brightly.

Shining Brightly as the Sun
Sharing Love with Everyone
Standing Tall for the Whole World to See.
They can Learn to Shine their Light
Just as Powerfully and Bright
For the Spirit in Them is the Same as the Spirit in Me.

How Brightly are you Shining today? What is it that is temporarily in your way, and what is your plan to leave it behind?

Suggested Exercise: Shine! Shine Again! Shine Brighter!

100 Voices

There are 100 voices in my head, all speaking their truth. Almost all of them are reminding me to be Grateful, Patient, Kind, Loving, and Wise. They are chanting their mantras and singing their songs of Strength, Peace, and Joy. I love their Positive Energy!

It has not always been so. When I was younger, most of them were shouting at me to Be Careful! There is Danger!, Danger!, Danger! everywhere. They told me I was unworthy and to work harder. Some of them even told me that God would torture me unmercifully if I didn't repent and beg for forgiveness for all of my evil, sinful ways. Those voices scared the crap out of me!

Slowly over time, those disparaging voices of my own thoughts have changed their tunes. One by one, the angry, frightened, discouraged, and shaming ones have been replaced by voices of Kindness, Confidence, and Patience. Slowly, they began to tell me that there was nothing to be ashamed of and that not only was I Worthy of Being Loved, that I *was* Loved – completely and unconditionally.

There are only five or six out of the 100 voices that are still speaking discouragement and fear these days, and they are mostly very quiet. I still hear them every once in a while, but not very often, not very loudly, and not very long. I forgive them, and thereby forgive myself, whenever I hear them.

Mostly, I hear the other 95 voices, reminding me, encouraging me to Remember, Embrace, and Become the Angel Within. They remind me of the Beauty of the Spirit, and how Sacred, Amazing, and Precious every moment of my Life really is.

More and more these days, I hear them telling me to Let Go and Love. They are encouraging me to step aside and let Spirit come through, and take this Life Experience to the next level.

And those are the Voices that are the most Intriguing to me now.

> *What are your 100 Voices saying to you? Are they shouting words of anger and danger, or are they reminding you of the Beauty of the Spirit? How have they changed over time?*
>
> *Suggested Exercise: When you hear your Voices today, encourage the positive ones to speak up, and tell all of the others to take a hike.*

The Vital Energies

The Vital Energies in my subconscious mind are reorganizing and expanding. They are:

The Loving Heart
- Acknowledgement, Respect, Acceptance, Appreciation, Admiration
- Support, Encouragement, Praise
- Forgiveness, Kindness, Tenderness, Mercy, Compassion
- Friendship, Generosity, Guidance, Nurturance, Embracement
- Reverence, Devotion, Service

The Joyful Spirit
- Light-Heartedness, Happiness, Playfulness, Silliness
- Laughter, Merriment, Amusement, Cheerfulness
- Eagerness, Enthusiasm, Excitement, Energy, Optimism
- Amazement, Wonder, Curiosity
- Freedom, Celebration

The Peaceful Presence
- Relaxation, Letting Go, Releasing, Surrendering
- Healing, Resting
- Calmness, Grace, Tranquility
- Stillness, Silence, Serenity, Bliss
- Listening, Feeling, Watching
- Opening, Blossoming, Becoming

The Wise Soul
- Detachment, Transcendence, Awakening, Awareness
- Remembering, Understanding, Seeing
- Consciousness, Clarity, Independence
- Truth, Knowingness, Certainty
- Fairness, Justice, Objectivity
- Authenticity, Integrity, Honesty, Transparency
- Gratitude, Humility
- Guidance, Intuition
- Oneness

The Powerful Warrior
- Patience, Poise, Confidence
- Health, Vitality, Vibrancy
- Faith, Trust, Security, Safety
- Vision, Intention, Choice, Decisiveness, Focus
- Planning, Preparation, Alignment
- Courage, Daring, Bravery, Boldness
- Action, Assertiveness, Passion, Force
- Working, Manifesting, Attracting
- Persistence, Determination, Tenacity, Commitment
- Will, Endurance, Perseverance, Strength
- Reliability, Dependability, Responsibility, Accountability
- Adaptability, Coachability, Flexibility, Resilience
- Transforming, Changing, Learning, Growing
- Allowing, Receiving, Embracing, Becoming
- Achieving, Accomplishing, Completing
- Honor, Pride

The Capable Professional
- Valuable, Capable
- Creative, Inventive, Imaginative
- Insight, Experience, Skill, Knowledge
- Talent, Intelligence, Brilliance
- Precision, Diligence, Thoroughness, Excellence
- Communication, Cooperation, Collaboration, Synergy
- Productivity, Efficiency, Effectiveness
- Eloquence, Artistry, Mastery
- Abundance, Prosperity

What words carry Life-Giving, Vital Energy for you? Do these words give you a little Zing?

Suggested Exercise: Read through the list when you want to Shift Your Energy in some way. Better yet, memorize it and repeat it several times a day.

Not Going There

There have been a couple of times in the past two weeks that I found myself hurt by the attitudes and words of other people. I was in a mindset of child-like innocence and vulnerability, hoping for praise and words of encouragement, and got aggressive questions instead. Ouch!

I'm not sure if they jumped on me or not. It could be that I was just super-sensitive, with "no shields up". I suspect it was a combination of the two.

I also suspect that being in that place was a variation on the defense mechanism of submission.

And my guess is that my submissiveness and "please love me!" victim energy attracted their aggressiveness.

Anyway, I'm Not Going There anymore.

I'm going to practice being Loving, Tender, Sweet, Open, and Kind without being too Vulnerable, without concern for the responses of others.

When was the last time your vulnerability was exposed? How did others respond to your innocence – did they embrace you or attack you?

Suggested Exercise: Practice being humble, loving, and kind, with child-like innocence, without vulnerability.

Independence

There appears to be a higher level than being Consumed by Love: Independence.

> Independence from **one moment to the next**,
>> So that how I felt and what I was thinking and doing just a moment ago has little or no bearing on what I am thinking, feeling, and doing right now.
>
> Independence from **the thoughts, feelings, and actions of others**,
>> So that the response of others to my presence has no impact on my own thoughts, feelings, and actions.
>
> Independence from **my own story**,
>> Such that my life's journey simply doesn't matter.
>
> Independence from **my own thoughts, feelings, and actions,**
>> So I am not attached to anything I am thinking, feeling, or doing.

All will pass.

All will pass away.

All are Beautiful, Amazing, and Precious.

And I Am Present.

How independent are you? How able are you to choose your thoughts, feelings, and actions independent from others and the moment that just passed?

Suggested Exercise: Practice independence today. Practice being the person you want to be, The Angel Within, no matter what is happening around you.

Always Sending Love

I have a new strategy for being Independent and Awakened – to meet Every Person, Each Thought, and All of My Feelings with a single, crystal Expression: Love.

If I am Always Sending Love,

> there is no room in my Consciousness for shadow energies such as weakness, regret, disappointment, or anger.

If I am Always Sending Love,

> there is only room for More and More Love, Flowing through Every Moment in Magnificence.

So I will focus on Loving Every Person, no matter what they say, feel, think, or do.

And I will focus on Loving Myself the same way.

After all, after I Recover, Remember, Embrace, and Become my Higher Self, I always end up Sending Love to the World in Every Way – why not just start there and stay there?

It's the Ultimate Proactive Courageous Positive Action.

How often are you Sending Love? How would it change your life if you were Always Sending Love?

Suggested Exercise: Practice Always Sending Love today. Make it a habit.

My Blind Spot

I can usually tell when I am not in the Spirit
>and when I am First In The Spirit,
>>but I am not very good at noticing when the Spirit is Fading.

I want to believe that I am still there,
>when I am not.

I allow myself to get distracted.

I have a Blind Spot.

My Ego wants to cling to My Higher Self, to squeal with delight and tell the world what I have achieved and rally them to experience it too!

But with that identification and that attachment, comes the Decline of Consciousness.

What a paradox – to be focusing completely on Being In the Spirit, while giving up all attachment to it. To Love it, Embrace it, but not desire it.

And the fact that it is temporary, makes it all the more Precious to me.

Time to check my Blind Spot.

What Blind Spot(s) do you have? When and how does the Spirit fade for you?

Suggested Exercise: Get in the Spirit. When you notice you are no longer there, figure out what the circumstances were when you began to descend. .

On Stage

A friend from a men's group remarked today that I was more personable and friendly when I met with him one-on-one and face-to-face than I was in when we were together in our group.

I sat with that for a bit, knowing, sensing that he was right.

I am grateful that he pointed out another Blind Spot.

It seems that when I am speaking in a group, I have a tendency to be on stage – I speak a little more assertively and artificially than I do when there are just two or three of us. I am just a little bit arrogant and insecure.

I am not sure why – probably some fear over the group turning hostile and de-pantsing me, tying me to a clothesline pole, or beating me up or something. I suspect there is some deep fear from my childhood long ago, coupled with my love for theater and getting applause from audiences of all sizes.

I sense that I have been "showing up tough" in an effort to impress them. Maybe I have been having a little Alpha Male energy so they won't turn on me.

My operational paradigm is to be tough, smart, and funny – On Stage – in order to protect myself.

It is humbling to see how fearful I have been.

When are you On Stage? When are you pretending and when are you Authentic?

Suggested Exercise: Practice being Humble, Open, Transparent, and Authentic today. In some way large or small, stop pretending.

Vibrational Variability

It is So Strange coming in and out of Higher Consciousness.

    I want to be at my Best More of the Time.

    I want to make my Best a Higher and Better Best.

    And every day, I Rise and Fall.

Like the Wind and the Weather,

    like the Tides and the Waves,

        my Consciousness Comes and Goes.

Over Time, I am Becoming.

    Becoming Wiser, Stronger, more Peaceful, more Loving, more Joyful... More in a lot of ways.

    And more Humble at my Vibrational Variability.

It's pretty Amazing, really.

Do you see yourself coming in and out of Higher Consciousness? Are you becoming Wiser, Stronger, more Peaceful, and more Joyful day by day?

Suggested Exercise: Practice your Awakening a few extra times today. Revel in the Process.

This Moment Too

This Moment, I Celebrate another Awakening.

This Moment, I set aside all resistance
  to My Transformation.

This Moment, I am Watching.
This Moment, I Remember.
This Moment, I am Independent.
This Moment, I am Amazed.
This Moment, I Choose.
This Moment, I Transform.
This Moment, I am Free.
This Moment, I am Silent.
This Moment, I am Powerful.
This Moment, I am Consumed by Love.

This Moment, I am Watching my Thoughts and Feelings. I am Transcending and Awakening.

This Moment, I see my Joy and Suffering from the same Dispassionate Perspective.

This Moment, I am completely Detached from what is happening, what happens next, and what happened previously.

This Moment, I Remember the Beauty of the Spirit.

> I Remember that when I am there, it is the most wonderful experience in the world.
>
> I Remember that I have Returned thousands of times, and I know that
>> I Can Again,
>> I Will Again, and that
>> I Am Returning Again.

This Moment, I see that this moment is Unique and like no other moment. I see that *This Moment* is Independent from all other moments, and that I am Independent from the thoughts, feelings, and actions of others, including myself.

This Moment, I am Amazed at this experience of life.

This Moment, I am Choosing and Transforming – consciously and intentionally, or otherwise.

This Moment, I am Free to be and experience whatever I choose.

> And I choose to be Powerful, Silent, and Loving
>
> I choose to be Consumed by Love.

This Moment, I see that my feelings are real, my thoughts are real, and this experience is real, even though they are quite fleeting.

This Moment is just one moment in the context of my lifetime.

This Moment is all there is.

This Moment.

(repeat)

Are you in The Moment right now? Have you stepped back from your current thoughts and feelings, or are you still attached?

Suggested Exercise: Think about this moment, then think about everything that has happened today, then the past month, then the past year, then your lifetime. See this moment in the context of uncountable precious and interesting moments.

Resistance

Strangest thing – I occasionally have some resistance and hesitation to Awakening. Sometimes, my head remembers the beauty of the Spirit but my heart resists going there.

Even though I have walked a path to My Higher Self thousands and thousands of times,

> Even though that when am I there, I just LOVE being there,
>
> Even though being Awakened is my favorite experience of all,
>
>> I still hesitate.

And I think I feel a little self-pity, a little "woe is me", instead of Rejoicing and Celebrating.

Then I sense that it could be that the Universe is just reminding me to not take myself so seriously.

So I Choose to laugh at myself and Awaken anyway.

Are you able to become your Higher Self whenever you want? Why do you hesitate?

Suggested Exercise: Practice, Practice, Practice Awakening to Your Higher Self.

The Great Turning

There is a moment when I begin to stop thinking about the challenges and issues I am facing,

> When I stop examining my darkness,
>> And I Turn Towards the Light.

Sometimes it is all at once – a complete and sudden "about face".

Sometimes it is gradual,

> Perhaps starting with a little awareness of something behind me,

And then I look over my shoulder,

Then I turn a little bit,

> And I see the Beauty that Awaits

So I turn a little more,

> And then a little more,
>> And so on.

This is My Great Turning.

Sometimes slow, sometimes fast.

> And Always Amazing and Wonderful.

How quickly do you usually Turn Towards the Light? Do you turn slowly or quickly? Once you Remember Again, how long does it take to Be There?

Suggested Exercise: Turn towards the Light Right Now. Embrace it, Become it, until It is All There Is.

The First Light of Joy

This morning I woke up several steps from Spirit.

When I checked in, I found that my body was tense, my thoughts were unfocused, my emotions were very flat and serious, and that I was barely conscious.

It took me several times through my This Moment meditation to Return to Spirit.

And along the way, I focused on Relaxing, Releasing, and Letting Go of the tension in my body.

I slowed down my thoughts and gained control of them again.

I remembered how Amazing this Experience of Life is.

I stepped back and saw my Morning Transformation in the context of so many other similar moments.

And then came that Wonderful, Beautiful Moment:

>The First Light of Joy.

Like a welcome candle in the darkness,

>the Joy returned to my Experience

>>and I began to Smile.

And I thought of how Precious a Gift my Joy is.

And I thought of all the other people in the world who were still caught up in their tension and their seriousness, and had yet to experience their First Light of Joy this morning.

And I wished that I could Share mine.

Have you had your First Light of Joy today? Have you shared it yet?

Suggested Exercise: Practice becoming Joyful as quickly as you can tomorrow morning and every morning for the rest of your life. Then Share Your Joy.

Excitement!

I woke up this morning with a feeling of Excitement – the Excitement of Life Unfolding.

I am Excited to see how this day turns out!

I am Excited to see how my conversations turn out – what will be said, what will be felt, what will be decided.

I am Excited to see the products of my work – what will be created, updated, and accomplished.

There are so many possibilities!

And I know that no matter what happens,

>   I will be Watching and Loving
>
>   with Excitement!

Are you Excited, too? Do you see how Incredibly Amazing and Wonderful this Journey of Life is?

Suggested Exercise: Practice Excitement and Amazement today. Share the Energy with others!

Barking Dogs

A vision came to me this morning when searching the depths of my soul.

There were a lot of dogs barking down there, trying to warn me of danger. They barked when someone criticized me, they barked when some disagreed with me, and so on.

I adopted each dog whenever something scary or painful happened in my life. I said to myself "wow, that is really scary – I think I'll get a dog to protect me and warn me of times when that could happen again. They will sense my fear before I do, and bark to warn me."

Now, there are Chihuahuas, Beagles, Bloodhounds, Dobermans, Pit Bulls, Labradors, and Mastiffs, all barking like crazy when something comes up that triggers them.

They are only trying to protect me.

So I am training them not to bark. When they bark I let them know that they are heard, that it will be OK, and I thank them for their service. Then I send them back over to the corner with a treat or a chew-toy, and they go back to sleep again.

I have a lot of appreciation and respect for my canine friends.

Do you have Dogs Barking in your subconscious mind, too? How many? What are they protecting you from?

Suggested Exercise: Examine all the little buzzes and barks you are receiving. Make a list of them. Focus on how you can quiet almost all of them just by feeling safe.

The Right Path

It occurred to me this morning that I approach the Return to Spirit from many places, including Desperation, Despair, Darkness, Determination, and Delight.

It has been a while since I was in a desperate place, but every once in a while I despair a little bit, feeling a since of lack. Sometimes the victim or prisoner energy comes back, usually in a very small way.

In those times, I am uncomfortable where I am, and I really want to change. My world just isn't "right", and I know there is a better place. And sometimes there is resistance and hesitation. I feel justified in my anger or my shame, and I don't feel worthy of anything else. It is like I simply choose to feel miserable for a little bit longer. But eventually, I let go of my resistance, tuck my tail between my legs, and humbly walk a path back to spirit.

When I am in the Pit of Darkness, the first challenge is Remembering the Light, and the second challenge is Believing that I can Return, and the third is Making the Decision to do so.

Other times, when I am not so stressed, I return out of habit and dogged determination. I am not particularly uncomfortable where I am, but I remember that there is a much better way to live. So I say to myself "hey, why not?" and I begin the process.

When I find myself to be in the Pit of Darkness or in the Shadows of Complacency, physical movement, such as stretching, walking, breathing can start the process of transforming. Then I start controlling my thoughts by simply counting slowly. Soon, the lethargy and stiffness dissolve, and I begin to focus on more advanced meditations.

And then there are those wonderful times when I am simply delighted to return! I remember how Beautiful Life Is when I am In the Spirit, when I have Returned to That Glorious Condition, and I happily focus on walking the short path back to Bliss.

There are many Approaches to Spirit, many paths home – the "right" one depends on where I am.

Do you Return from many different places? Do you have an approach to Returning no matter where you are?

Suggested Exercise: Make a list of ways you can Return when you are in the Pit of Darkness, and ways you can Return when you are already Mostly In the Light.

Even Though

Even Though there are times when I feel a bit like a victim or a prisoner,

Even Though there are times when I feel a little unworthy,

Even Though there are times when I am somewhat afraid,

> I am Still Willing to Believe that I can be and will be
>
>> A Great Spiritual Teacher.

Even Though these past few years have been challenging financially,

Even Though I am not sure of what I want to do next,

> I am Still Willing to Believe that Abundance and Prosperity will flow into my life
>
>> Easily and Gracefully.

Even Though I was not in the Spirit a few moments ago,

Even Though I was in the Pit of Darkness or Trapped in the Shadows,

> I am Still Willing to Believe that I can and will return to that Glorious Condition
>
>> Quickly and Joyfully
>>
>> Right Now.

What is holding you back? What is blocking your success? Are you Willing to Believe that you can accomplish your dreams and live a marvelous life "even though"?

Suggested Exercise: Name the things that are holding you back and create your own "even though" meditation. Practice it and you will be free!

Wonderful and Amazing

Returning to the Spirit

> Is always More Wonderful and Amazing than I think it is going to be.

Even though I have Awakened 30,000 times,

> It is still always More Beautiful and Precious than I Remember.

It is like the difference between thinking about diving into cold water and the experience of it.

It is like the difference between imagining a loving embrace and being in the arms of a lover.

The imagined experience is not the same as the real experience.

But unlike physical experiences,

> Imagining the Spirit
>
> And Remembering the Spirit
>
>> Is the doorway to the Experience.

I wrote about it many years ago in my *Remember* message:

> *And here is an amazing truth: if you Remember the Spirit within you strongly enough, you will experience it again. You will be at your best again, every time…*

And so I will humbly Remember

> that I cannot Imagine
>
>> how Glorious my Next Awakening will be.

Do you find that the Return to Spirit is often or Always more Amazing than you thought it would be? Do you wonder why you ever hesitated?

Suggested Exercise: Imagine and Pretend that your Return to Spirit will be more Amazing and Wonderful than you thought it would be. Then Return.

I Will Not

I will not be discouraged because I still get discouraged.

I will not be angry with myself because I still get angry from time to time.

I will not be afraid of my own fear.

I will not be ashamed of my embarrassment, my guilt, or my shame.

It is one thing to feel these things, and it is quite another thing to continue feeling them
> When I know I have the Power to Let Them Go.

Are you ever embarrassed to be embarrassed, ashamed to feel ashamed, or angry over being angry?

Suggested Exercise: The next time you sense a negative energy, don't throw fuel on the fire! Instead, step back and learn the lesson.

Perspectives on Transforming

I find that I have a lot of different perspectives on transforming, depending on my Level of Consciousness.

Some of them are as follows:

- Already there!
- Joyful Celebration
- Relaxed and Eager Pursuit
- Committed Focus
- Hesitant Tip Toeing
- Indecision
- Consideration
- Resistance
- Refusal
- Defiance
- Unconscious Ignoring

What is your Perspective on Transforming? Are you Already There? Have you totally forgotten the power you have to Transform for a few minutes?

Suggested Exercise: Next time you Remember that you have Transformed in the past and can Transform again, make a note of your starting place.

Watching Triads

Watching, Freezing, Panicking,
Watching, Screaming, Fighting,
Watching, Arguing, Blaming,
Watching, Grieving, Crying.

Watching, Worrying, Stressing,
Watching, Resisting, Defending,
Watching, Despairing, Withdrawing,
Watching, Struggling, Searching.

Watching, Standing, Deciding,
Watching, Daring, Competing,
Watching, Focusing, Acting,
Watching, Doing, Achieving.

Watching, Considering, Allowing,
Watching, Relaxing, Trusting,
Watching, Forgiving, Accepting,
Watching, Aligning, Quieting.

Watching, Smiling, Chuckling,
Watching, Remembering, Seeing,
Watching, Releasing, Opening.

Watching, Listening, Breathing,
Watching, Blossoming, Awakening,
Watching, Embracing, Becoming,
Watching, Loving, Being.

Watching, Supporting, Inspiring.

What are you watching yourself doing right now? What Triads have you experienced today?

Suggested Exercise: Check in with yourself several times today. Make a note of what you are experiencing.

This Time

This Time, it was not my Blessing to be born wealthy or powerful.

This Time, it was not my Blessing to be born a Master or win the Spiritual Lottery.

This Time, it is not my Blessing to be constantly Awakened and Consumed by Love.

This Time, it is my Blessing to be Healthy and Vibrant.

This Time, it is my Blessing to be Intelligent.

This Time, it is my Blessing to have a Wonderful Family.

This Time, it is my Blessing to be Humble.

This Time, it is my Blessing to Overcome my Fears

    Slowly

    Day after Day after Day.

This Time, it has been my Blessing to Awaken

    Thousands and thousands of times

        So that I might learn to help a few others find a way to Awaken, too.

And I am Grateful for My Life

    This Time.

What is your life experience This Time? What are your Blessings this time around?

Suggested Exercise: Make another list of your Blessings, This Time. Refer to it often.

Even Though II

Even Though I am Imperfect

> I am Still Willing to Believe in my Strength
> I am Still Willing to Believe in my Wisdom
> I am Still Willing to Believe in my Love.

Even Though my friends, my family, my clients, and my colleagues are imperfect, too

> I am Still Willing to Love them and Believe in them
>
> I am Still Willing to help them see the Glory and Presence that lies within each of us.

Even Though there are those who would blame me for their lack

> I am Still Willing to Believe that we are each Responsible for Our Own Lives
>
> And that together, we Manifest our Shared Reality.

Do you believe in yourself despite your imperfections? Do you believe in others, too? Do you see the Presence in each of us?

Suggested Exercise: Make a list of the ways you screwed up yesterday and the times you judged and criticized others. Then burn it.

Beyond Transcendence

I woke up this morning with a Level of Transcendence that was beyond that which I had experienced before.

I Transcended my Transcendence.

I stepped back and saw my life, my journey with complete passivity

> Not desiring,
>
> Not needing,
>
> Not wanting to be anything, do anything, or have anything else.

Just content with the life I have experienced and the road that has been travelled.

I don't need to be a Spiritual Teacher, a gazillionaire, or anything else.

It is a librating place

> Beyond Transcendence.

Where the only things left

> are Love
>
> and Games.

What do want to do, want to be, and want to have? Are you still desiring and wanting things and experiences?

Suggested Exercise: Imagine what it would be like to be completely beyond any desire, living totally in the now.

Thousands of Times

I woke up this morning
> as I have done over 20,000 times.

I Meditated and Elevated My Consciousness
> as I have done over 30,000 times.

Looking back,
> I have been angry thousands of times,
>
> Frustrated thousands of times,
>
> Anxious, nervous, and worried thousands of times,
>
> Peaceful thousands of times,
>
> And Joyful thousands of times.

I have judged and criticized others 10's of thousands of times,
> And I have Forgiven and Loved them just as often.

These days, it seems that no matter what I am experiencing,
> I have experienced something quite like it
>> Thousands of Times before.

And each time I wake up in the morning

And every time I Awaken,
> I am Amazed at Being Alive.

Have you Awakened and Forgotten thousands of times, just like me? Have you been anxious and loving, attached and detached, thousands of times, too?

Suggested Exercise: Make a list of the things you have done 10's of thousands of times. There's a lesson in the list for you.

I've Been Here Before

It seems like every time I Awaken these days

    Even just a little bit

        I have the deep sense that I have been here before.

I have been in this state,

    With the same amount of tension and stress

    With the same amount of
    Love and Consciousness

        Thousands and Thousands of times.

I've seen movies like this thousands of times before:

    they all have a beginning, a middle, and an end.

Maybe that is what the next level of detachment is like:

    an awareness of the current moment

    in the context of so many other moments.

And I see that at each moment, I had a choice.

        I could choose to Remember, Embrace, and Become the Angel Within

    Or I could choose to be complacent

        and simply slip back
        into Unconsciousness and Attachment.

In retrospect,

    It is quite humbling to see

    That I have not chosen to move into Spirit

    Nearly as often as I have chosen otherwise.

But Right Now

    I choose Spirit.

Are you Present in This Moment? Do you see This Moment in the context of your lifetime?

Suggested Exercise: Step back and see This Moment in the context of the millions of moments you have experienced so far, and hopefully, the millions of moments you will experience this time around.

Checking In

I check in with myself many times a day.

And it is humbling to report that even after doing so thousands and thousands of times,

> I still experience times when there is a lot of resistance and hesitation
>> to Returning to Spirit.

I don't feel safe letting go of my thoughts.

I don't feel safe changing the focus of my attention

> to My Higher Self.

And it is the level of resistance and hesitation that shows me how far in the shadows I am.

The less I feel like Letting Go, Releasing, and Loving,

> The deeper in the Shadows I have gone
>
> And the more Wonderful and Amazing the Return always is.

Always Is.

Always Is.

And still I forget and I hesitate.

And then….

> I Remember to Love Myself again.

Do you check in with yourself many times a day? Are you humbled by the times you forget to commit to Spirit?

Suggested Exercise: Check in Now. Awaken Now. Return to Spirit Now. Then do it again with every breath and every heartbeat.

Fear

Fear is so interesting.

We have it when we are born,

> And it grows throughout our lives
>
> Into many forms and manifestations.

It is there to protect us.

> It keeps us from burning ourselves, playing with things that hurt us, getting hit by cars, and so on.

And so it becomes the great inhibitor

> Holding us back from doing things that are really not dangerous at all
>
> Such as speaking in public, auditioning, selling, and such.

And we seem to crave it

> With our games and our competiveness.
>
> Why else would we jump out of planes, ride roller coasters, and watch horror movies?

And yet,

> It is the very thing
>
> That separates us from Spirit.

Fear,

> The great protector,
>
> The great inhibitor,
>
> The great entertainer / exciter,
>
> The great separator.

Awesome…

Now it is time to set it aside completely
    And just Love.

> *Have you studied your fears lately? Do you see how your fears protect you, inhibit you, and excite you? Do you see how they separate you from Spirit?*
>
> *Suggested Exercise: Spend a few minutes examining your fears without getting caught up in your fears. Analyze them. Study them. Then let them go and do sometime joyful!*

Vision Star

I woke up this morning with a new vision of what my Life Intentions are.

My new Vision Star is:

Just focusing on it helps me feel Grounded and Clear.

Are your Intentions Grounded and Clear? Do you have a diagram that helps you Focus?

Suggested Exercise: Create your own Vision Star with the five things most important to you.

The Dawning of Consciousness

Here I am again,
> at the Dawning of Consciousness.

For some reason, I just Woke Up again, just a little bit.

I have been here many thousands of times before.

And I know that I have some choices:
> I can go back to sleep,
> or I can continue to Stay Awake
>
> I can Move Towards Spirit,
> or I can stay where I am.

....

I know that it is safe
> to Let Go of my thoughts
>> and Return to Spirit.

And it seems that all of these messages were created
> just so I could Have a Reason
>> and Find a Way to do so.

My rational, analytical, ego mind just needed something that made sense
> Some way to organize and align the Energies in my Attention
>> So I would feel safe in Letting Go
>>
>> So I would feel safe Allowing
>>
>> So I would feel safe Receiving.

And I find that the Depth of my Fear is Amazing.

And the Magnificence of a Life Without Fear
> Is Really Quite Astounding.

> *Are you at The Dawning of Consciousness? Do you feel safe in Continuing to Awaken?*
>
> *Suggested Exercise: Take a minute and Awaken. Know that you are Safe. Experience life with no fear for a while.*

The Choice

I Choose to Believe with Absolute Certainty

> that my Entire Life is a Manifestation of my Subconscious Mind,
>
> a Perfect Reflection of my Inner Being,
>
> and I Accept Complete Responsibility for Everything I See, Feel, and Experience.

I Choose to Believe with Absolute Certainty

> that my Evolution is an "Inside Job",
>
> and I Know that I do not Manifest that which I Think and I Desire at the Conscious Level -
>
> I Manifest that which I Am.

So with All of my Heart

> And from the Depths of my Soul

I Choose, I Request, I Allow, I Accept, and I Embrace

> an All-Consuming Union with Spirit.

With All of my Heart

> And from the Depths of my Soul

I Choose, I Request, I Allow, I Accept, and I Embrace

> Powerful, Joyful, Loving Relationships with Everyone and Everything
>
> Especially Myself.

With All of my Heart

    And from the Depths of my Soul

I Choose, I Request, I Allow, I Accept, and I Embrace

    Amazing Opportunities to Share my Wisdom and my Love

    In ways that Divinely Inspire, Empower, and Heal others.

With All of my Heart

    And from the Depths of my Soul

I Choose, I Request, I Allow, I Accept, and I Embrace

    Fantastic Wealth and Abundance

    In Every Way and for All Time.

And with All of my Heart

    And from the Depths of my Soul

I Choose, I Request, I Allow, I Accept, and I Embrace

    Dynamic Health and Vitality Every Day

    until the End of Time.

For I live in a Magical, Mystical Universe.

And I Choose to Believe with Absolute Certainty

    that my Entire Life is a Manifestation of my Subconscious Mind,

    a Perfect Reflection of my Inner Being,

    and I Accept Complete Responsibility for Everything I See, Feel, and Experience.

I Choose to Believe with Absolute Certainty

> that my Evolution is an "Inside Job",

> and I Know that I do not Manifest that which I Think and I Desire at the Conscious Level -

> I Manifest that which I Am.

And so It Is Done.

And so It Is Done.

And so It Is Done.

Amen.

What do you believe? What do you Choose, Request, Allow, Accept, and Embrace?

Suggested Exercise: Create your own Prayer of Becoming and repeat it several times a day.

My Voices

Just in the past few days, I have Discovered and Embraced some very distinct Voices in my Soul:

- The Voice of Authority – confident, certain, with absolute knowingness
- The Voice of Leadership – commanding, focused, driven, powerful
- The Voice of Wisdom – quiet, inviting, enlightening, brilliant
- The Voice of Joy – inspiring, releasing, energizing, invigorating
- The Voice of Humility and Gratitude – gentle, open, soft-spoken, authentic, transparent
- The Voice of Love – compassionate, comforting, supporting, healing, and peaceful

They are more powerful than they have ever been.

And now I am practicing

> Choosing the Right Voice
>
> for the individual and the situation.

What Voices do you have? What Voices are you Choosing to Use?

Suggested Exercise: Practice using the Voices in Your Soul. Choose the one you feel is appropriate and Focus all of your energy on Being the Person You Choose to Be.

Thank You Spirit

Thank You Spirit.

I am Grateful for the many times I have been Consumed by your Presence

 For the Union I am Experiencing Right Now

 And for the Certainty of Living the Rest of my Life

  In an Ever-Increasing Union with You.

We are Becoming One.

Thank You Spirit.

I am Grateful for the thousands of Joyful, Loving Relationships

 I have experienced

 And am Enjoying Right Now

  Especially the times I have been Completely in Love with Myself.

I look forward to Embracing Everyone,

 Every Time, and All of the Time,

 For the Rest of my Days.

Thank You Spirit.

I am Grateful for the many Opportunities I have had to Share my Love and my Joy

 In ways that Divinely Inspire and Heal others.

I am Grateful for the Opportunity I am having Right Now

> And for the Millions of Opportunities I will have in the days to come.

Thank You Spirit.

I am Grateful for the Fantastic Abundance I have experienced in my life

> For the Incredible Abundance I am experiencing Right Now
>
> And for the Wealth and Abundance I will experience today, tomorrow, and forever more.

Thank You Spirit.

I am Grateful for the Tremendous Health and Vitality I have experienced in my Life

> For the Powerful, Positive Energy flowing through me Right Now
>
> And for the Blessing of Health and Vitality in the years to come
>
> Every day until the end of time.

Thank You Spirit.

For these and for all of the Blessings I have experienced

> I am experiencing
>
>> And I will experience in my Life.

I am most Grateful.

Amen.

> *What blessings are you thankful for? What are your intentions for the rest of your days?*
>
> *Suggested Exercise: Using the framework of this meditation, create your own version with intentions that are especially meaningful to you. Memorize it, and repeat it several times a day for a while.*

The Flip

The common known responses to a frightening situation are to Fight or to Flee. This is often referred to as the "fight or flight" response.

A less common known response is to Freeze.

But there is still another tactic I use, and that is to Flip.

With the Flip, I simply do two things:

- I turn off the darkness as I would Flip a light switch on. Sometimes it is a little slower, as with a rheostat, but the Light comes on, and the darkness is gone. Without the fear, there is no reason to Fight, Flee, or Freeze.

- I Flip my perspective and see the fear as a blessing and a gift, and find the lesson in the fear.

Most of the times, there are lessons in Humility, Gratitude, and Faith.

And I am reminded of my Power and of the many ways I have learned to Return to Spirit, and I Remember that I get to experience the Joy of Returning again. What a Blessing!

So just Flip!

What are your typical responses to fear? Are you an argumentative person? Do you shrink away from conflict or do you just freeze?

Suggested Exercise: Next time you sense a bit of fear, try to Flip. Have an immediate change of perspective, and see the fear as an opportunity to practice your self-control and learn a lesson.

Becoming

May we each continue to become More of the Time

>That which we gloriously manifest
>Some of the Time

>>And truly are All of the Time...

Spirit.

How often do you manifest that which you truly are? Do you sense Spirit within you right now?

Suggested Exercise: Memorize and repeat his mantra silently whenever you are with others – and smile!

The Blessings of Humility

A few months ago I gave in to the universe, realizing that God must really want me to learn the Lesson of Humility,

    Because I kept receiving so many reasons to be so.

In other words, I have been screwing up in ways large and small all my life.

There have been tremendous accomplishments to be sure,

    But still, perfection in all ways has eluded me. ☺

So, in my men's group, I let go of being called "Jaguar" and became the "Humble Hamster".

    "Humble" because that is what I chose to embrace,

    And "Hamster" because, well, it is hard to take myself seriously when my animal totem is a hamster.

What I have found is really quite a Blessing.

In learning to show up Vulnerable,

    as if I were alone with my Best Friend

    or having a conversation with my most Trusted Teacher

        I find myself expecting to be Loved, Accepted, and Supported.

By Embracing Humility:

    I see my mistakes quicker and thereby learn from them more quickly

    I am able to examine and own my weaknesses and shortcomings without fearful resistance

    I love myself and others more deeply

I feel more authentic and peaceful, and somehow, wiser.

And like so many other lessons I have learned

I am humbled by the time that it has taken to learn it.

Are you a Humble person, or are you still somewhat Arrogant? Do you see the difference between Humility and weakness?

Suggested Exercise: Think about the Powerful yet Humble people you know. Meditate on how you feel around them. Practice being like them.

Action and Adventure

I watched a couple of very exciting and entertaining movies the last couple of days.

You know – the kinds where there were a lot of gunshots, explosions, fires, blood, death, and mystery.

Stories where the bad guys do bad things, innocent people get hurt or worse, and the hero emerges injured but victorious.

They were very exciting!

And then, last night, I had crazy, fighting dreams. I was deceived by friends and had to shoot my way out of a trap. It seems like the exciting, negative energy of the movies made its way into my subconscious.

Or, perhaps, from the metaphysical perspective, the negative, fearful energy from my subconscious became manifest in the form of movies.

In either case, it seems a bit unhealthy -

> This addiction to excitement...

Are you addicted to excitement, too? In what ways does that show up in your life? Are you also addicted to drama and stress?

Suggested Exercise: Make a list of all the things you do to feel excited. Think about how an addiction to excitement, in you or in others, has caused problems or brought great benefits.

Joy Walking II

Last year I wrote about Joy Walking, how I was walking down the street and came into a State of Being where everything I saw or heard triggered a Joyful Response.

Now, I am into:

- Joy Greeting, Joy Leaving
- Love Breathing, Peace Breathing
- Peace Walking, Power Walking
- Grace Working, Happy Working
- Power Moving
- And more….

It is fascinating the power we all have to program our responses to everyday things.

It is humbling to reflect on how most people don't even try.

Are you intentionally programming your subconscious mind, or are you just accepting your current responses?

Suggested Exercise: Take note of a simple response you have to a non-threatening stimulus, such as a train whistle or an airplane flying overhead. Intentionally program yourself to think Joyful Thoughts whenever it happens.

Fireflies

I remember times when I was growing up in Kansas where, on warm summer evenings, there would be dozens, or perhaps hundreds or thousands of fireflies in the yard. We kids would try our best to catch them and put them in jars for a while, so we could continue to watch their magic.

And it occurs to me now that I am like one of those fireflies – flitting around with my light shining now and then, all the while focusing on shining my light a little brighter and a little more often. My goal is, of course, to shine like the sun all of the time.

But for now, I find it somewhat amusing to think of myself and others as fireflies.

Trying our best to let our little asses shine. ☺

Do you shine from time to time like a Firefly? Can you turn yourself on and off whenever you want?

Suggested Exercise: Shine! Shine Again! Shine Again!

I Am

I am, I am, I Awaken, I am.
I am, I am, I Remember, I am.
I Awaken, I Awaken, I am, I am.
I Remember, I Remember, I am, I am.

I love, I love, I Awaken and love.
I love, I love, I Remember and love.
I Awaken, I Awaken, I love, I love.
I Remember, I Remember, I love, I love.

I see, I see, I Awaken and see.
I see, I see, I Remember and see.
I Awaken, I Awaken, I see, I see.
I Remember, I Remember, I see, I see.

I laugh, I laugh, I Awaken and laugh.
I laugh, I laugh, I Remember and laugh.
I Awaken, I Awaken, I laugh, I laugh.
I Remember, I Remember, I laugh, I laugh.

I Awaken to the Awareness of Who I am.
I Remember the Splendor of Love.
I See with Amazement this life that I lead
And I Laugh with great Joy from above.

Are you Awake right now? Do you Remember right now? Are you Consumed by Love right now?

Suggested Exercise: Repeat this little poem a few times. Awaken. Remember. See. Laugh!

An Eight Step Path

I Awaken.

I Remember.

I Relax.

I Re-turn.

I Smile.

I Love.

I See.

I Am.

I Awaken. Once again I am Opening My Eyes at the Dawning of Consciousness. I Detach and Look Out at this Amazing World.

I Remember.
1. I Remember that there is a beautiful place called Spirit.
2. I Remember that Spirit is almost always more magnificent than I Remember or Imagine it to be.
3. I Remember that I have been there thousands and thousands of times, and that I can and will go there again. I know that by thinking these thoughts, I am already on my way.
4. I Remember that the longer it has been since my last Awakening, or the more hesitation and resistance I am having, the more wonderful this Awakening will be.
5. I Remember that there are thousands and thousands of ways to get There.

I Relax. I Let Go of my tension. I Release my stress. I Quiet my Mind. I Embrace the Silence.

I Re-turn. I turn again towards the Light and I Focus on It. I continue to Walk a Path and Return.

I Smile. I little Smile comes over my face. I Chuckle and perhaps Laugh a bit at the Incredible Beauty of Life.

I Love. I Love Myself, Everyone, and Everything. Love Pours through me out and into the World.

I See. I See Myself and Everyone from the Context of my Lifetime, through the Eyes of an Angel.

I Am. I Am my Higher Self, Spirit, The Angel Within, One with Source and the Energy of the Universe.

What path are you walking today? Are you open to walking another path right now?

Suggested Exercise: Try this!

The New Remember

I Remember
- The Place
- The Challenges
- The Paths
- My True Nature
- My Power
- The Experience
- Wisdom.

I Remember The Place.

1. I Remember that there is a beautiful place called Spirit, even though I am sometimes so far away that it seems like a myth or a fairy tale to me, and I even forget that I have ever been there.

2. I Remember that Being In The Spirit is almost always more magnificent than I Remember or Imagine it to be.

3. I Remember that the longer it has been since my last Awakening, or the more hesitation and resistance I am having towards my Return, the more wonderful this Awakening will be.

4. I Remember the Angel, the Presence, and the Greatness that is within each of us.

I Remember The Challenges.

1. I Remember that when I am in the shadows and attached to my current thoughts, feelings, and perspectives, it is very easy to forget that Spirit even exists.

2. I Remember that I have many habits of lower consciousness that must be set aside in order for me to Experience Spirit.

3. I Remember that I often falsely believe that I am trapped in my current consciousness.

4. I Remember that I often falsely believe that I am safer in the shadows or even in the pit of darkness than I am in the Light.

5. I Remember that it is difficult for me to stay In the Spirit, and how I constantly slip back into lower consciousness without realizing it.

6. I Remember that I am easily distracted and lose my awareness of Spirit. It happens when I am working, talking with others, watching TV, and so on – whenever I am focused on other things.

7. I Remember the Six Gremlins of lower consciousness (Fear, Forgetfulness, Attachment, Complacency, Unconsciousness, and Unworthiness) that often combine to delay my Return to Spirit.

8. I Remember my subtle addictions to Approval, Excitement, Drama, Stress, Thinking, Cleverness, Doingness, Control, Possessions, and Self-importance, and the way these addictions often slow down my Return.

9. I Remember that it is difficult to stay in the Spirit when I am thinking.

10. I Remember that personality transplants often take a long time.

11. I Remember that it is as difficult to detach from Joy and Excitement than it is from stress and suffering.

I Remember The Paths.
1. I Remember that I have walked a Path to Spirit thousands and thousands of times.
2. I Remember that I can and will go there again, and I know that by thinking these thoughts, I am already on my way.
3. I Remember that there are many, many ways to get there, and I only need to walk one path right now.
4. I Remember that by Practicing my Awakening, it gets easier and easier to walk a path many times a day.
5. I Remember that while many paths have been valuable, no path is truly necessary.
6. I Remember that all paths, even this one, have limited application.

I Remember My True Nature.
1. I Remember that I am Spirit having a Human Experience.
2. I Remember that I am a Drop of Consciousness in the Sea of God's Mind, living an Illusion of Separateness and Mortality.
3. I Remember that in my Highest Expression, I Am the I Who is Perfect. I am not only the Do-er and Watcher, but the Dreamer-Creator, too. Simply, I AM.

I Remember My Power.
1. I Remember that I have the Power to Choose to Return to Spirit any time I want.

2. I Remember that when I am There, I see that my True Power and Potential is a thousand times greater than what I have manifested so far.
3. I Remember the Power I have to remind others of the Spirit, of the Presence within each of us.
4. I Remember the Power I have to help others find a path that is comfortable to them, so that they might also Remember, Embrace, and Become The Angel Within.

I Remember The Experience.

1. I Remember that when I am there, when I am In the Spirit, I am filled with incredible Peace, Joy, Strength, Wisdom, and Love – all at the same time!
2. I Remember the Beauty of Silence, the Healing Power of Bliss, and the Glorious Rapture of Joy!
3. I Remember how Amazing it is to be alive!

I Remember Wisdom.

1. I Remember that everyone, no matter how strange or ill-chosen their attitudes and behaviors, is just trying to be happy and to protect themselves. They are trying rescue themselves from their own fear and darkness as best they can.
2. I Remember that I can be In My Bliss when I am working.
3. I Remember that I can be In My Bliss when others are not.

4. I Remember that I never have to worry again. I never have to complain, whine, be angry, or be afraid, ever again. I can Live in the Light.

5. I Remember that while I may slip back into the Shadows from time to time, I never have to stay there. I can and will Return to Spirit very quickly, every time.

6. I Remember that I am Living in the Light, Consumed by Love, more and more every day.

What is important for you to Remember? Make a list.

Suggested Exercise: Read this every morning for a few days.

The Responses

There are many possible perspectives and responses to life's problems, as follows:

The **Victim's** Response:
- I was treated unfairly, and this situation was not my fault. There was nothing I could do about it, and there is nothing I can do about it. My situation is hopeless, and I can only whine and cry.
- Motto: Leave me alone!

The **Prisoner's** Response:
- I am trapped. I cannot escape. There is nothing I can do, and I am mad as hell!
- Motto: I Rage.

The **Tyrant's** Response:
- I will crush those who oppose me, and impose my will on the world. I will badger and belittle others, maybe even abuse or imprison them, until the situation changes.
- Motto: I Rule.

The **Child's** Response:
- It wasn't my fault! I was doing my best, but I'm just a kid.
- Motto: Don't Blame Me!

The **Manager's** Response:

- I will get others to do what I need them to do; if they do not fall in line or contribute to the team as I want them to, I will replace them. No Problem.
- Motto: I Control.

The **Salesman's** Response:

- I will persuade others to change their attitudes and behaviors so they will do what I want them to do. I may be kind and gentle, or I may be harsh and brutal, but I will be persuasive.
- Motto: I Persuade.

The **Hermit's** Response:

- If others bug me in any way, I will withdraw and find another path to happiness. Instead of changing the situation, I will change myself.
- Motto: I Am Self-reliant.

The **Sorcerer's** Response:

- I see that this situation is of my own making, a manifestation of who I am. I will see the blessing and learn the lesson, thereby reducing or eliminating the chance that this will happen again.
- Motto: I Manifest.

The **Student's** Response

- I see this is a learning opportunity. I learn what I can, and I am grateful for the lesson.
- Motto: I learn.

The **Teacher's** Response:

- I see this situation as an opportunity to teach others and help them learn valuable life lessons.
- Motto: I Teach.

The **Friend's** Response:

- I will encourage and support others, through the good times and the bad.
- Motto: I Support.

The **Cheerleader's** Response:

- I believe in you! I see your greatness and know that you can win. Get back up! Go for it!
- Motto: I Encourage.

The **Colleague's** Response:

- This is an opportunity for teamwork. I will work with others to find an agreeable solution for all and get the job done.
- Motto: I Collaborate.

The **Angel's** Response.

- I will love you totally and completely. There is nothing you could ever do that would cause me to stop loving you.
- Motto: I Love.

How are you responding to the people in your life? How are they responding to you?

Suggested Exercise: Pick one of these responses and practice it for a while.

In The Light

I walk In the Light.
I work In the Light.
I play In the Light.
I rest In the Light.

I speak From the Light.
I love With the Light.
I live In the Light.

I Am the Light.

> *How much Light do you have in your Life? Are you walking, talking, living, and working In the Light?*
>
> *Suggested Exercise: Memorize this little poem and make it your mantra today.*

Healing Tears

I was privileged to attend a weekend retreat with a men's group this past weekend. We have been meeting for a while, and have very strong and open connections.

I learned a lot about myself that weekend.

I learned that there are many levels of pain:

- The pain we acknowledge and openly reveal (sometimes dwelling upon it)
- The pain we acknowledge and only share with a few and / or only some of the time.
- The pain we acknowledge only to ourselves and don't share at all, often times denying it to everyone.
- The pain we deny even to ourselves.
- The pain we don't even know about.

In my childhood, big boys didn't cry, brave men soldiered on, and poets were not nearly as popular as cowboys.

We never learned the healing power of tears.

In my experience, there is great value in being Humble and Vulnerable, of daring to examine that which scares us the most and hurts us the most. In doing so, it is helpful to be able to cry.

It takes a lot of courage.

It takes a lot of support.

It takes a lot of honesty.

It takes a lot of self-love.

And when the pain has been discovered, exposed, and shared,

       the tears can flow and the healing can begin.

Best done in the company of strong friends.

> *When was the last time you dared to touch one of your own nerves? When was the last time you had the courage to cry?*
>
> *Suggested Exercise: In the company of strong friends, dare to find and expose your deepest fears. Cry and be healed.*

Magic Storeroom

There is a Magic Storeroom in my soul, where

> Everything I want to be, I Already Am
>
> Everything I want to do, I Am Already Doing
>
> Everything I want to experience, I am Already Experiencing.

And everything I want to have is there for me,

> to Choose, Take, Select, Pick Up, Embrace, and Consume
>
> > Whenever I Remember.

I see all of these packages arranged in a nice little circle, in three sections, and I am standing right in the middle.

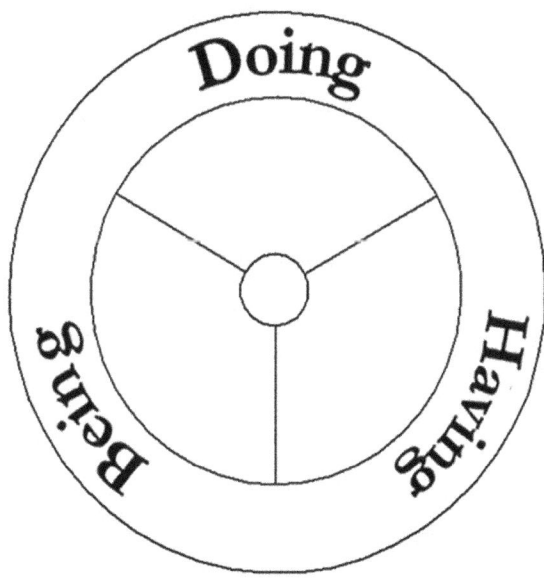

In the **Being** section, there is:
- The Angel Within
- The Watcher in the Stillness
- The Dreamer-Creator
- The "I Who is Perfect"- "The Great I AM"

In the **Doing** section, there is:
- Being a Leader, an Elder, a Shaman, and a Sage
- Being an Consultant, Manager, Entrepreneur, and Tycoon
- Sharing (Speaking, Writing, Singing, Mentoring, Supporting)
- Spiritual Teaching
- Experiencing Nature (Walks, Hikes)
- Analyzing (Projects, Spreadsheets, Programming, Accounting)

In the **Having** section, there is:
- Prosperity (Being in an Easy Massive Flow of Financial Abundance)
- Freedom and Independence
- Health and Vitality
- Home and family
- Relationships and Tribe

It is all there, just waiting for me

    to Choose, Take, Select, Pick Up, Embrace, and Consume

        Whenever I Remember.

What is in your Magic Storeroom? Do you see the power of knowing that everything you have always wanted, you already have?

Suggested Exercise: Make a list of the things in your Magic Storeroom. Practice being them every day for awhile.

60

Today is my 60th Birthday and it feels like a Victory!

I am healthy and happy with wonderful family and friends and the energy and enthusiasm of a much younger man. Wahoo!

And here is my thought for today:

> "I choose to be at my best today in every way, and love myself totally and completely, whether I am at my best or not!"

In my experience, the best way to live life is to be consumed by Love and Joy and Bliss. And the only way I have found to love others totally and completely is by loving myself totally and completely, and vice versa.

Love is a state of being and a gift, not a request.

So despite our flaws and weaknesses, and even though we all have lessons to learn and a ways to grow, I choose to love US, totally and completely.

Today and every day.

Forever.

Did you celebrate your last birthday? How young do you feel? Do you understand that Love is a State of Being?

Suggested Exercise: Meditate on the ways in which withholding Love from others is also withholding Love from yourself.

Variations on a Theme

I choose to be at my best right now, and love myself totally and completely.

I choose to be at my best right now, and love myself and others totally and completely.

I choose to be at my best today, and love myself totally and completely, whether I am at my best or not!

I choose to be at my best today in every way, and love myself totally and completely, whether I am at my best or not!

I choose to be at my best today in every way, every moment of the day, and love myself totally and completely, whether I am or not!

I choose to be At My Best today

> in every way,
>
> every moment of the day,
>
> and encourage others to do the same.

And I choose to Love us all today

> Totally and Completely,
>
> whether we are at our best or not!

Are you choosing to be at your best today? Are you choosing to love yourself and others even when you find that you have not been at your best?

Suggested Exercise: Practice Loving Yourself and Everyone Else Totally and Completely today. Get real good at it!

Energy Shivers

I have been getting Energy Shivers for many months now. Sometimes I just lay in bed and shiver for 30 seconds or more, but most of the time they come and go in a second or two.

And they always offer some stress relief – my body feels more relaxed and aligned immediately after experiencing one.

And I have come to see them as signals from my subconscious or superconscious mind that I am on the right track. They are the universe's way of telling me "yes".

They happen a lot these days – many times a day, whenever I am meditating or just thinking.

What a blessing it is to have that signal!

Others use pendulums and dousers, or they do some muscle testing. I am not sure why, but I have not practiced those techniques yet.

But the Energy Shivers – they are undeniable and very welcome.

Are you being signaled by the universe in some way that you are on the right track? Do you get warning messages, too?

Suggested Exercise: Find a way to get a "yes" from the Universe or your subconscious mind. Practice using it.

The Dreamer-Creator

I choose to see myself as the Dreamer-Creator of my life.

And as The Dreamer-Creator:

- I accept total responsibility for everything I see, feel, and experience as a manifestation of my subconscious mind.

- I understand that when I hold others responsible for my experience in any way, I am giving away my power.

- I believe that life is one big puzzle, the end game of which is coming to understand my true nature as the Dreamer-Creator so clearly that I am able to create the life of my choosing.

- I choose to see every experience as a lesson and a blessing, as another clue to the great unraveling, as another opportunity to learn and grow.

- I set my intentions and focus my attention knowing that the things I want to be, do, and have, are already mine.

And so it is.

Do you see yourself as the Dreamer-Creator of your life? If so, how are you using that mindset? If not, do you see the possibility?

Suggested Exercise: Practice embracing the mindset of the Dreamer-Creator. Envision the future you would like to experience. Focus on it Completely. See it being true. Then act in a way that is consistent with that belief.

I Forgive Myself

I see myself being unconscious, and I forgive myself.

I see myself forgetting the Beauty of The Spirit, and I forgive myself.

I see myself being complacent, and I forgive myself.

I see myself being a little embarrassed, and I forgive myself.

I see myself being a little nervous, and I forgive myself.

I see myself being stressed out, and I forgive myself.

I see myself thinking too much, and I forgive myself.

I see myself getting angry, and I forgive myself.

I see myself whining and complaining, and I forgive myself.

I see myself forgetting the power I have, and I forgive myself.

I see myself making poor choices, and I forgive myself.

I see myself making mistakes, and I forgive myself.

I see myself feeling unworthy, and I forgive myself.

I see myself being critical of myself, and I forgive myself.

I see myself being critical of others, and I forgive myself.

I see myself failing to immediately forgive myself, and I forgive myself.

And I see myself thinking that I need to forgive myself, and I forgive myself.

All is forgiven.

And I am Free.

> *Do you hold any regrets or resentments? Who do you need to forgive?*
>
> *Suggested Exercise: Practice forgiveness today. Start with forgiving yourself for one regret you have been holding onto. Then forgive someone else and let go of a resentment.*

Do Unto Others

It is becoming clearer and clearer to me that the Golden Rule is a little mis-phrased.

Instead of "do unto others as you would have them do unto you"
> I think it is more appropriate to say:
>> "as you do unto others, so you do to yourself".

I call this "The Law of Consistent Energy".

When I judge others harshly and condemn them in some way,
> I am also judging and condemning myself.

When I withhold my Love from others in any way,
> I am limiting the Love that I experience in my life.

When I do not forgive others,
> In some way large or small
>> I am refusing to forgive myself.

For it is only by Loving others Totally and Completely
> That I can Love myself Totally and Completely.

It is only by Forgiving others without reservation
> That I can entirely Forgive myself.

And you can be assured that this moment
> I Love You
>
> Totally and Completely.

What are you doing unto others that you would not have them do unto you?

Suggested Exercise: The next time you judge someone, think about how you are really judging yourself.

Humility II

Being open to Humility has been helpful to me in many ways.

Some of the biggest reasons for my Humility are:

- When I am silent, I can see and feel what is going on in my subconscious mind. I feel the energy shift when someone walks into the room, when a commercial is played on TV, and when a song starts. When I was thinking all the time, my attention was just on my thoughts. Seeing the depth of my childhood fear and understanding the challenge of reprogramming at the deepest levels of who I am is a very humbling experience.

- I see what a remarkable challenge it is for me to break the habits of lower consciousness; of being attached to my thoughts, feelings, and experiences instead of watching them from afar while I am sensing them. Even though I have developed the ability to change my consciousness in a matter of minutes no matter what, it is very humbling to see that I continue to live in the Ego, instead of in the Spirit. I do not always live In The Spirit, even though I know that I could.

- It takes the pressure off. In some way, I don't have to be perfect anymore. I don't have to care what others think of me. I can go about my business of being, sharing, doing, and experiencing, without regard to "their business".

It is a fine thing, this virtue and practice of Humility.

Are you a Humble person? Are you too frightened to become one?

Suggested Exercise: Sit in the silence as best you can, and sense the workings of your subconscious mind.

Staying Awake

Now that I can Remember, Return, and Become The Angel Within so easily,

Now that I have done it 30,000 times,

> it is time to change my focus;
>
>> Because for each of the times I have returned,
>>
>>> I have also drifted away.

Awakening is no longer an incredible challenge - it is always a blessing and mostly easy to do.

Staying Awake is the challenge, for I am still easily distracted by thoughts, work, and conversations. They are Shadow Magnets and Distracters.

My thoughts from the Spirit are supportive and entertaining,

> But then the energy of my thoughts changes without my awareness
>
> I become attached to them
>
>> And I slip back into the Shadows.

My work is very exciting and seems to require all of my attention

> But then my addictions to Approval, Control, and my own Cleverness begin to take hold
>
> I become attached to my work
>
>> And I lose my focus on Spirit.

Conversations, whether in writing, over the phone, or in person, seem very important

And I quickly forget all about Being in the Stillness

As I become attached to the interaction.

There are other distractions, of course, but these are the big three:

Thoughts.

Work.

Conversations.

And I think this is a significant turning point in my Spiritual Growth:

Discovering and Reducing

the Shadow Magnets and the Distracters.

What causes you to drift away from your own Higher Consciousness? Are you also distracted by thoughts, work, and conversations?

Suggested Exercise: Make note of the times today that you fell out of The Spirit and what caused the separation.

Being Awake

After a day of focusing on Staying Awake, I learned a valuable lesson:

> It isn't about Staying Awake at all.
>
> It is about Being Awake.

For me, the term "Staying Awake" carried with it some negative energy.

There was a fear of drifting back into unconsciousness,

> and a bit of self-criticism for not being permanently In the Spirit.

And here's my lesson:

> The Diligence of Consciousness must be undertaken with a Light and Humble Heart,
>
> With a Celebration of Awakening and Awareness
>
>> Instead of ruing the lack of perfection.

My cup is 99% full.

I am very Grateful.

And is definitely Time to Party!

> *Are you celebrating the Light or cursing the darkness? Are you grateful for your progress or despairing over the work that remains?*
>
> *Suggested Exercise: Make a list of your accomplishments and blessings – then celebrate them!*

Energetic Momentum

The energy in my soul is self-perpetuating.

> I am happy because I am happy.
>
> I love myself because I love myself and love others.
>
> I feel strong because I feel strong.
>
> And so on.

On the flip side, the negative energy has momentum, too.

> I am ashamed that I feel embarrassed.
>
> I am angry that I am angry.
>
> I am upset that I am upset.

Allowing the positive energy to gain momentum is a very good thing.

Interrupting and stopping the momentum of the negative energy
> is the key to shifting that energy from negative to positive.

Where do you find Energetic Momentum in your life? Are you cruising down a blissful highway or sliding down a slippery slope?

Suggested Exercise: List three ways to keep the positive energy flowing and three ways you can interrupt the momentum of negative energy.

Anxieties

There are so many ways of being afraid! Here are just some of them:

- **Decision Anxiety**: The fear of making a bad choice.
- **Mistake Anxiety**: The fear of making a mistake.
- **Commitment Anxiety**: The fear of putting all (or a lot) of your eggs in one basket, because of the risk of disastrous consequences.
- **Over-Commitment Anxiety**: The fear of committing too much and failing in one or all of your commitments as a result.
- **Dependence Anxiety**: The fear of becoming dependent on a person, a job, or anything else, because of the risk to being cast aside or let down.
- **Focus Anxiety**: The fear that you are going to miss out on something cool because you are paying too much attention to something else.
- **Relaxation Anxiety**: The fear of letting go for fear you will miss something or be in danger in some other way.
- **Inception Anxiety**: The fear of getting started in a way that messes you up.
- **Performance / Execution Anxiety**: The fear of not being able to do the work on time and /or correctly.
- **Completion Anxiety**: The fear of having an unsatisfactory outcome – or – the fear of the change that accompanies the completion.

- **Criticism Anxiety**: The fear over someone disapproving with your choice, your actions, or your opinions.
- **Rejection Anxiety**: The fear of being shunned or cast out.
- **Confrontation Anxiety**: The fear of getting hurt / shamed / embarrassed while fighting.
- **Trust / Friendship Anxiety**: The fear of being let down or deceived.
- **Authenticity Anxiety**: The fear of being yourself and speaking your own truth (and being ridiculed or rejected as a result).
- **Control / Authority Anxiety:** the fear of being in charge and screwing it up.
- **Weakness Anxiety**: the general fear of being too weak, and being unable to protect yourself.
- **Change Anxiety**: the general fear of the unknown.
- **Failure Anxiety**: the general fear of being judged a failure by yourself and others.

I have experienced all of these in my life, and still do in some measure from time to time. Sometimes, I encounter several of them at the same time.

Facing them has been a very humbling process.

I now know that all of my anxieties are just attempts to protect myself, created long ago by a very young and small little kid. I had no choice, no power over my subconscious condition back then.

But I do now.

Now, my choice is to Admit my anxiety, Forgive Myself, Love Myself Anyway, and Move On.

And I am not afraid to do that.

Are you facing any anxieties in your life right now? Are you willing to admit them, forgive yourself, love yourself, and move on?

Suggested Exercise: The next time you are a little tense or downright scared, examine the flavor of your anxiety for a few minutes. You might ask yourself how you came to have that fear. But most importantly, Remember that you are not trapped, and that you can Let Go and Return to Spirit – Right Now.

Feeling, Thinking, and Requesting

One of the challenges that many people have is expressing their concerns. They let things bottle up until the stress manifests as an explosion or a disease.

I know I had the problem for a long time.

But I have recently created a very effective way of expressing concerns, following this simple three step formula:

1. I am **uncomfortable** about this situation. This is what I am **feeling**. (A "heart" statement)

2. I am **concerned** that left unresolved, the consequences could be troublesome. This is what I am **thinking**. (A "head" statement)

3. This is my **request** of you in this situation. This is the **action** I would like to see happen – OR – this is my **decision** and the **action** I am going to take. (A "hands" statement)

Try it the next time something bugs you. Tell the person involved directly and simply what you are feeling, what you are worried about, and what you would like to have.

It works.

Do you have a simple process to manage conflict and express your concerns? Are you withholding a lot of opinions and suggestions out of fear or just not knowing how to express yourself?

Suggested Exercise: Try this process! It really works!

Flavors of Bliss

I was recently in Hawaii, where I just love the beaches. It felt great to swim in the warm ocean water and relax to the sound of the waves on the shore.

The big lesson for me on this trip was that the Bliss of the Ocean was not in any way better than the Bliss of the Mountains or the Bliss that I experience in other situations – it was just another, wonderful flavor of Bliss.

And I know at a deeper level than before that my Bliss doesn't really depend on where I am or what I am doing –

>it only depends on the amount of fear I am experiencing.

The Bliss while lying in bed completely relaxed and refreshed,

>the Bliss while taking a walk,

>the Bliss while just sitting in silence, etc.,

>>are all equal in their Blissness.

And my opportunity is to increase the circumstances under which I am willing to be Blissful,

>to allow myself to experience The Spirit whether I am surrounded by nourishing places in nature

>>or in the hustle and bustle of city life;

>whether I am completely Silent and Relaxed,

>>or tired and in pain, and so on.

Does your Bliss depend on being in a particular place or with a certain person? Does it depend heavily on your external circumstance? What do you need in order to experience Bliss?

Suggested Exercise: Make a list of all the places you have experienced Bliss and who was with you (if anyone). Are there any common themes? Practice not being so dependent on your external circumstances.

The Icing or the Cake?

There are many who look at the Spiritual aspects of life:
> Connecting to Source,
> Living a life of Love and Gratitude,
> Becoming the Angel Within,
>> as icing on the cake.

To them, they are Nice, but not Necessary.

What feeds them is their cake:
> earning money,
> managing a career,
> accumulating possessions,
> connecting with the rich and famous,
> doing things and having things.

But for me, Being In the Spirit is the cake**,** and the rest is just fluff. It is interesting, but not really that important.

My life would never be complete or meaningful without Spirit. It is the Beingness, not the Doingness or the Havingness, that is most important to me.

But my first choice is a wonderfully delicious piece of German chocolate cake (with extra coconut, please!) – with plenty of scrumptious icing.

What is the cake and what is the icing in your life? Are you focusing so much on the cake that you never taste the icing or vice versa?

Suggested Exercise: Make a list of the things that are really important to you. Note the ones that are most important (the cake), and ones that are just fun (the icing).

The Amazing Bliss of Beingness

A few days ago I wrote about the Many Flavors of Bliss, and yesterday, that perspective went to a whole new and wonderful level.

I spent the day finding the Bliss in Everything.

It didn't matter what I was doing. Managing email, bookkeeping, chores, watching TV, eating dinner, etc., all were the same.

I found the Bliss in every life experience – every action, every thought, every breath, and every heartbeat. I even found the Bliss in the little hassles of everyday life, things that would normally give me a little buzz of stress – instead, they were just more reasons to be Blissful.

This morning, there was the Bliss in waking up, the Bliss in making coffee, the Bliss of turning on my computer, the Bliss of sitting in the silence, and the Bliss of writing these words.

It was, and it continues to be, a simple, easy, and wonderful choice to make.

It is such a beautiful thing, this Amazing Bliss of Beingness.

Can you imagine the beauty of being propelled into Bliss by every experience in your life? What would that mean to you? Can you imagine being in a perfect state of Bliss all of the time?

Suggested Exercise: Purposefully expand the circumstances under which you allow yourself to be Blissful today. And then do it again tomorrow.

Sherry's Book

My lovely wife has her own spiritual path, although she would never call it that.

Mine is gentle; hers is a little more direct.

Here it is:

Chapter One: Get Over It

- Dwelling on the past does not heal you. It hurts you. Do your best to work through any painful memories, acknowledge them, and get over them.

Chapter Two: Focus on the Now

- Once you have stopped dwelling on the past, in turn, don't worry about the future. Focus on the now and enjoy every glorious moment.

Chapter Three: Let It Go

- Hanging on to your painful story helps no one, least of all, yourself. Just let it go. Replace it with a less painful story.

Chapter Four: Rise Above

- Don't be a victim of your circumstances. Rise above them. Learn from them and move on.

Chapter Five: The Past is a Bucket of Ashes

- Those painful memories are not treasures. Throw them away, or better yet, spread them on the ground and grow some flowers.

Chapter Six: Don't Make the Same Mistakes

- Do you make mistakes from time to time? Have you made mistakes in the past? So what? Learn your lessons from them and do your best not to make those same mistakes again.

Chapter Seven: Move On

- You don't have to totally ignore the past, but it helps to focus on today and have hope for the future. It can be very bright indeed. Move forward. Move on.

Chapter Eight: Help Others

- Take time to put your own struggles aside and help others. It's a win-win experience! Both of you will benefit and everyone needs a little help from time to time.

Chapter Nine: Do Your Best

- Give yourself a break when you aren't the best. Just keep trying. Do *your* best, as often as possible.

Chapter Ten: Hurry!

- I know you have a lot to do. Hurry!

What pain are you holding on to? How is that serving you? Have you considered just getting over it and moving on? Does that scare you?

Suggested Exercise: Get Over it. Let it Go. Move On. Hurry!

Bliss List I

I decided to make a list today of all of the things that brought me Joy, focusing once again on the opportunity I have to make every situation and every experience fuel for my Bliss Factory.

Here's a list of the things that triggered my Bliss today:

- Waking up and remembering the opportunity I have to be in my Bliss
- Breathing and thinking
- Going to the bathroom
- Weighing myself and discovering I was still a few pounds heavier than I wanted to be
- Having a cup of coffee
- Reading email, especially the one where a prospect said he was ready to become a client
- Playing a couple of games of Snood
- Taking a shower
- Singing a silly song in the shower
- Making a smoothie concoction
- Beginning this list
- Talking with Sherry about her new book
- Working with my partner, JP
- Exploring the many flavors of consulting
- Having Energy Shivers
- Stretching and popping my back
- Keeping track of my time

- Having a second cup of coffee
- Drinking my morning smoothie concoction
- Working on selling my house
- Making phone calls to old friends and new ones
- Looking out my window
- Being a little tense thinking about a phone call with an ex-client
- Spending a few minutes in the stillness and silence
- Having a soft-drink.
- Completing a challenging email.
- Having a turkey sandwich for lunch, while watching a little TV
- Singing a little song while cleaning up and preparing for visitors
- Getting back to work
- Talk to two old friends about our Bliss and the promise of 2012 (yea!)
- More chores
- Talking to visitors
- Eating potato chips
- Getting back to work
- Taking a dinner break
- Getting back to work
- Having a wonderful conversation with a new friend
- Solving a technical problem and completing a new web page

- Doing a little yoga
- Lying down for the night in a comfortable bed.

It's not so much that things *are* beautiful; it is that *I choose to see them as* beautiful, and I choose to see everything as fuel for my Bliss Factory instead of my crap factory.

And it was only my fear that caused me to do anything else.

What things trigger your Bliss and bring you joy?

Suggested Exercise: Make a list!

Bliss List II

Here's a list of the things that triggered my Bliss today:

- Waking up at 4:30 AM and remembering the opportunity I have to be in my Bliss today.
- Focusing on the Stillness and the Silence.
- Remembering that everything I want to be, do, and have is already mine.
- Remembering that what I want most is to be The Angel Within – to embrace Spirit so completely that I become Spirit.
- Remembering that nothing separates me from Spirit – that I am Spirit and always have been.
- Remembering that I could write this list.
- Noticing a little burp from the crap factory and chuckling.
- Getting a cup of coffee.
- Reading some emails.
- Playing a little game.
- Reading some more emails.
- Exploring the crazy sound problem in my wall!
- Listening to some beautiful music.
- Letting go of a little tension around a confusing relationship.

And then, unexpectedly, I slipped out of my Bliss for a few hours. I had a time of low energy and low level tension, until I woke up again and returned. The experiences that fueled my return were:

- Listening to Boston and singing at the top of my lungs on the way to class.
- Being in a class and learning a lot.
- Having a wonderful conversation with a good friend thereafter. His encouragement to help people focus on becoming who they wanted to be was just wonderful.
- Having a chocolate treat.
- Lying down in a warm soft bed.

This life is such a fascinating experience!

What things trigger your fear and your anger? Do you sometimes just slip out of your Bliss without realizing it?

Suggested Exercise: The next time you slip out of Bliss, note when and how it happened. Make a list, and then do something to counteract it.

Empowering, Relaxing, and Awakening

This little matrix about the Levels of Consciousness I experience throughout the day popped into my head as I awoke this morning. I spend more and more time at the Conscious level these days: working, writing, observing, and just having fun. I also still spend a lot of time being unconscious, a little time being tense and stressed, and upon occasion, I feel a bit trapped or weak.

The message of the chart for me was that I Empower myself to Build My Energy, I Relax to let go of my tension, worry, and stress, and I Awaken to move into Higher Levels of Consciousness, where I really like to live.

Conscious Energized Worker	Conscious Counselor Philosopher	Conscious Transcendent Observer	Conscious Cheerful Gamer
↑ Awakening ↑			
Relaxed Unconscious Worker	Relaxed Unconscious Talker	Relaxed Unconscious Vegetable	Relaxed /Unconscious Gamer
↑ Relaxing ↑			
Serious Worker	Intense Debater	Impatient Waiter	Intense Gamer
↑ Empowering ↑			
Lethargic Procrastinator	Disinterested and Hopeless	Depressed & Withdrawn	Giving Up & On the Bench

They don't have to happen in that sequence: sometimes I Detach, Transcend, and Observe my stress or pain, and then I Relax.

And now,

It is time to focus again on Empowering, Relaxing, and Awakening.

It is time to Remember the beauty of Strength, Stillness, and Consciousness.

Do you Elevate Your Consciousness and Shift Your Energy with a series of thoughts? Does this simple sequence work for you?

Suggested Exercise: Try this simple three step path: whenever you sense that you are not at your best, then Remember your Power, Relax, and Transcend. Be Strong, Silent, and Wise.

Blessed Beyond Measure

I woke up this morning with a realization that I have been off my game for a few days – experiencing a little less Bliss and Joy, while being a bit anxious and a little quick-tempered.

So I made a mental list of the things that were bugging me:

- **Physically**: my weight is up a few pounds, I tweaked a muscle in my leg, and I have been hungry because I'm eating less. I could use more exercise and a little more sleep.

- **Work**: I am behind on a couple of projects, not really sure what this month's income will be, and am working on a dozen large opportunities, not knowing which one(s) will come through. And I am working on rebranding myself and introducing some new products and services. I have a lot on my plate.

- **Financially**: I am getting ready to exit my current condo and move somewhere else, and am not sure when that will happen or the effort it will require.

- **Spiritually**: Being off my game takes me off my game; there is a bit of a downward spiral effect. I somehow feel a little bit less glorious. ☺

… and so on.

And then I Woke Up to and Remembered the many blessings in my life, and once again became aware that these little things were, well, little things – in no way could they limit my Bliss unless I allowed them to.

So I wrote this little mantra, and repeated it many times:

> Even though there are some little things that bug me right now, I am still Blessed Beyond Measure and I am Exceedingly Grateful for this Incredibly Beautiful Experience of Life.
>
> Even though there are some little things that bug me right now, I know that I can and will Return to Spirit as richly and deeply as ever before; that I can quickly come back into My Bliss and stay there.

It is always humbling to forget the Power I Have to Choose

> and oh so wonderful to Remember!

Do you have some things that are bugging you right now? Are you choosing to allow them to limit your bliss?

Suggested Exercise: Make a little list of your challenges, then set it aside and Return to Spirit.

The Fear of Life

A very long time ago, I went to a church that did their best to put the fear of God into everybody, to frighten them into obeying the rules, accepting the doctrine, and staying in the church community.

The alternative, so they said, was an eternity of hell-fire and damnation, of being tortured mercilessly by your loving Father.

It was a tough message to understand and believe.

And it was equally challenging to deny, because nearly everyone I looked up to, nearly every authority figure in my life bought into that crap, or at least, condoned the teaching.

And I came away with a temporary fear of God, and a very long lasting Fear of Life.

I am still healing that wound. There is a scar in my soul over that one.

I have forgiven them, of course. Like Jesus, I understand that they did not know what they were doing, that they were just trying their best to rescue themselves and me from the darkness.

They just totally screwed it up. They confused emotional abuse with Spiritual teaching. They condemned instead of loved – just like they had been taught to do when they were children.

The blessing for me has been a lifetime of figuring things out for myself, and coming to discover the Presence within each of us, of learning to Love others in spite of their apparent shortcomings.

And for that, I am truly Grateful.

Were you taught to be fearful when you were young? Are you still fearful? Have you found a healthier, less stressful path to walk?

Suggested Exercise: Think about the ways in which your current spiritual community spreads negative energy through condemnation of others or in any other way. Choose to believe and act with Love, instead.

I Do

I suspect that there are people who never feel any stress or anxiety in their lives.

    But I do.

There may be others who never get worried, who never get angry, and who never get nervous or upset.

    But I do.

Perhaps some folks never feel even a little bit unworthy and never feel like they could use a hug.

    But I do.

Maybe there are a few incredible advanced souls who never forget the Presence, the Divine Spark within each of us.

    But I do.

And because I do, I find great value in a smile, a word of encouragement, and a tender moment. I love it when people remind me of how beautiful I can be.

Do you?

Are you perfect? Do you expect yourself or others to be? Do you somehow judge yourself to be unworthy because you are not?

Suggested Exercise: Be the best you can be right now. And Love Yourself completely. Always.

Tree Hugging

A long time ago, I heard about the glorious redwood trees in California. I knew they were tall and mighty, but didn't pay much attention. I thought the tree huggers were a little wacko in the way they worshipped them.

Then I moved to California and found myself one day at the foot of one of the oldest and largest ones in Basin State Park. And as I stood at the base of this 14 foot in diameter, 200 ft tall, 2,000 year old tree, I was smitten. I was completely mesmerized at the grandeur, the magnificence, and the beauty of this incredible living thing. I could feel its energy, and it was Amazing. I even put my arms out and embraced it as best this little body could.

In an instant, I became a tree hugger.

And so it has been with Spirit, with this wondrous State of Being I have learned to Love. At first, experiencing Enlightenment, Awakening, and Higher Consciousness was but a nice story, and then I found myself one day falling madly, eternally, and completely in Love with Spirit as I approached it. Then I embraced Spirit as best I could, and experienced The Angel Within.

In one instant, I became a Spirit-hugger for life.

And so my wish for everyone else in the entire world is that they also find their way to the Presence Within.

Because when they do, I know when they will become a Spirit-hugger, too.

Have you ever hugged a tree? Have you ever hugged Spirit?

Suggested Exercise: Meditate on the biggest most wonderful thing you have ever experienced or ever hope to experience. Imagine that it is Spirit, and you are embracing it as it embraces you.

Imagining My Life

Today, as I spent a lot of time in the Stillness observing my State of Being, I reflected:

> The ego is a little tense, but Spirit is not
>
> The ego is somewhat tired, but Spirit is not
>
> The ego is a bit worried, but Spirit is not
>
> The ego is slightly embarrassed, but Spirit is not
>
> The ego is a tad upset, but Spirit is not...
>
>> ... and I am Watching it all.

Once again, I seem to be three creatures at once: the Ego, the Spirit, and the Watcher of both.

And every once in a while,

> I sense that I am the Dreamer – Creator, too
>
> Making all of this up
>
> Imagining my Life.

How many of you are there? Do you ever sense multiple points of view simultaneously? Do you both experience and observe at the same time?

Suggested Exercise: Go into the Stillness and watch for a while.

The Gush

Lately these days, whenever I feel a little buzz of anger, resentment, insecurity, embarrassment, nervousness, stress, or some other shadow energy, I activate The Gush.

> I Flood myself with Love and Kindness.
>
> I Pour the waters of Peace and Joy over my head.
>
> I Drink an elixir of Wisdom and Strength.

It almost never feels right when I start doing it, but I do it anyway. My inclination, my momentum is towards staying attached to my negative energy because I am frightened to let go of my thoughts and feelings. I almost always have some level of resistance towards The Gush, but I have learned to trust my Practice, and just do it.

I don't dwell on the shadow energy,

> I just let it go as quickly as I can.

The Gush is Healing.

The Gush is Transforming.

The Gush is Empowering.

And in that way,

> every little buzz becomes fuel for My Bliss Factory.

Do you some way to quickly reverse negative / shadow energy whenever you notice it?

Suggested Exercise: Next time you notice a little buzz (or a big one!), activate The Gush.

Just the Right Thing

I used to be fearful and competitive. Caught up in a scarcity mindset, I was worried that there was not enough business to go around, and that I wouldn't get my share.

But the ice has melted.

At first, I rationalized that if a person wanted to do business with one of my 'competitors', then I didn't want to do business with him. Maybe this was a little of a 'sour grapes' mentality, but I reasoned that my competitor's energy and services were so different from mine, that the odds were pretty good that I would not be able to have a good relationship with the client.

Then I heard that the lost prospect had a great relationship with my competitor. He was exactly what she needed! The transaction was completed satisfactorily for both parties.

As I sat with this, I learned an extremely valuable lesson:

    I am not right for everybody.

And I really can't tell what you need next –

    I can offer a solution,

        propose a piece of the energetic puzzle,

            but it is up to you to decide.

And I trust that you will make a great decision!

Are in a scarcity mindset? Do you get upset when someone chooses to go in a different direction? Have you seen times when people chose differently from you and still had a great result?

Suggested Exercise: The next time someone chooses to do something that is not apparently in your favor, focus on knowing that a perfect relationship is just around the corner, and wish them the very best.

The Other Side of Fear

I had a dream last night in which I was advising the president of the United States on an issue regarding technology funding.

I was not afraid. I delivered my opinion passionately and respectfully, with no attachment to the outcome.

And I realized that I had come to live on the Other Side of Fear for many days. I had been that person for the past week.

Clear. Passionate. Respectful. Supportive. Kind. Decisive. Masterful.

Humble. Grateful. Loving. Wise.

Experiencing a different, more powerful Flavor of Spirit.

After spending much time living in my Bliss, I sense that I am stepping into my Power.

On the Other Side of Fear.

How much fear do you experience in your life? Have you ever been on The Other Side of Fear?

Suggested Exercise: Make a list of the times you are able to be completely without fear – not just courageous, but completely without fear. Focus on being there many times today.

Hurry!

One of the things I love about my wife is that whenever I tell her that I have a lot to do, she immediately replies "Hurry!"

No pity party allowed. No sense of overwhelm allowed. No whining allowed.

Just focus and get the job done.

It works every time.

Do you whine and moan sometimes? Does it bring you any value?

Suggested Exercise: The next time you feel like complaining, just hurry instead!

Purposeful Breathing

I was talking with one of my spiritual teachers yesterday, and he encouraged me to take deep breaths, focusing on specific energies during the expansion (intake) and the release.

My experience, however, is that deep breaths don't work for me when meditating – it is only very shallow, relaxed breathing that elevate my vibration.

For him, it was the opposite: he connected deeper with Spirit with deep breaths.

So I began to explore the different types of natural and purposeful breathing I experience:

- Survival breath
- Recovery breath
- Energizing breath
- Focusing breath
- Normal breath
- Relaxing breath
- Stillness breath
- No breath

Each one has a purpose, and each one is exactly the right choice from time to time.

What kind of breathing do you experience in your day? Do you intentionally shift your pattern from time to time?

Suggested Exercise: There is great power in breathing! Practice some of these patterns for yourself today.

Base Camp

I have been meditating this past week with the simple questions: "If I were to receive Guidance right now, what do I imagine that Guidance would be?" or "If I were to receive a message from the Angels right now, what would that message be?"

For the first several days, the answer was always the same: "Return to the Stillness."

And so I did, 10-15 times a day, for many days.

Then the answer changed a bit. The response became: "Return to the Stillness, and then go further. Go 10-20% further than you thought about going".

And I did that for a few days.

Then the answer changed to: "Think of the Stillness as a Base Camp. There remains a marvelous journey ahead. Look upwards and continue."

And so I am.

What is your base camp? What State of Being, mindset, or mood defines your normally accepted condition? Is it as high up the consciousness trail as you want it to be?

Suggested Exercise: Practice returning to your 'best condition' time after time for a few days. Then go further.

Five Choices

At this Moment of Awakening,
> at this Dawning of Consciousness,
>> I know I have Five Choices.

First, I can choose to Love myself Totally and Completely,
> regardless of what has happened before,
>> regardless of what will happen in the days to come,
>>> and regardless of the remaining choices I make right now.

Second, I can choose to Remember or Imagine How Beautiful Life Can Be:
> I can Remember what it is like to Be In The Spirit
>> or I can simply remain forgetful.

Third, I can choose to move in the direction of Spirit,
> To detach and transform,
>> or I can simply stay where I am
>>> or go back to sleep.

Fourth, I can choose to go all the way to Spirit,
> Or I can just go part of the way.

And Fifth, I can choose to walk a path to Spirit
> Easily, Quickly, and Cheerfully,
>> or I can move slowly with some resistance and grumpiness.

This time, Right Now,
> I choose to Embrace Spirit,
>> To Become the Angel Within
>>> Easily, Quickly, Cheerfully, and Completely.

How about you?

What choices are you making right now about Spirit? Are you Awakening Easily, Quickly, Cheerfully, and Completely?

Suggested Exercise: Make the Five Choices several times today. And always choose to Love Yourself Totally and Completely, no matter what other choices you make.

Buzzes, Zings, Fogs, and Lamps

As I watch myself more and more often these days, I find it useful to note the Buzzes, Zings, Fogs, and Lamps.

- **Buzzes** are those things that bug me; thoughts and events that trigger my fear in some way, large or small.

- **Zings** are those things that thrill me; thoughts and events that trigger my joy.

- **Fogs** are like shadows that cling to me; they dull the zings and seem to enhance the buzzes. They may be just a light mist that is barely noticeable, or so thick that I am surrounded by darkness.

- **Lamps** burn away the fog; they dull the buzzes and enhance the zings. When the light is bright enough, there is no fog and only a few small buzzes.

What a freakin' fascinating Life!

Do you have Buzzes, Zings, Fogs, and Lamps in your life? Which are you experiencing right now?

Suggested Exercise: Focus some time and energy today on the things that bug you, thrill you, slow you down, and excite you. Work towards experiencing more Zings and Lamps!

The New Deal

I made a New Deal with Spirit today, with the Captain of the Team of Angels Surrounding and Supporting me:

I will supply the body and the voice, and they can supply the Wisdom, Strength, Peace, Joy, and Love.

In a new partnership, we will co-create a marvelous Presence and Energy to share with the world. We will help a lot of people and have a lot of fun in the process.

My part is pretty easy.

And they are pretty good at theirs.

What is your current deal with Spirit? Are you in charge, or is she?

Suggested Exercise: Try letting Spirit flow through you a few times today.

The New Assessment

I came up with a new assessment today that I am using every time I Awaken. Here it is:

1. What **preceded** the Awakening?
    a. If there was a Trigger, was it a Zing (joyful) or a Buzz (painful)?
    b. If not, was there something else that triggered the Awakening?
2. What is the **current state**? Where on the continuum of Bliss and Stress am I?
3. What is the level of **Clarity and Consciousness**? How detached and self-aware am I? Am I in the Fog or the Sunshine? Am I completely awake or partially asleep?
4. What is the **activity** level?
5. What is the **environment**? What is going on around me?
6. What **transformations** am I experiencing right now?

Most often, I find that some physical movement and a change in location precedes an Awakening Moment. It happens a lot when I get up to go to the kitchen.

Other times, it was an Energy Shiver or just glancing out the window that triggered the Awakening.

And still other times, it was the end of a phone call or a task of some kind.

Any Energy Shift can serve to trigger an Awakening. And often, the bigger the shift, the bigger the Awakening.

What triggers you to Awaken? Do you just meditate on schedule, or do you Awaken throughout the day?

Suggested Exercise: Use this new assessment for a while. Become more self-aware.

Celebration!

I Celebrate and Embrace a Deepening Connection to Spirit…

>Every Day
>
>Every Moment
>
>Right Now.

I am Open and Eager to experience a Greater Presence…

>Every Day
>
>Every Moment
>
>Right Now.

I am Focused on doing anything and everything I can to Strengthen My Awakening…

>Every Day
>
>Every Moment
>
>Right Now

… for the rest of my Life.

Are you celebrating a growing connection to Spirit, too? Are you Open and Eager to experiencing a greater presence? Are you Focused on your Awakening?

Suggested Exercise: Celebrate! Every time you think about this amazing life we share today, Celebrate!

New Rules

I have been playing Bakers Game for several years. It is a game of solitaire I find engaging and relaxing. On my old phone, I won about 20% of the time, which made me feel good about myself, because the instructions said that most people won about 10% of the time. ☺

When my old phone died and I got a new one, I quickly found a new version of the game. With this one, I could pick to play only games that could be won, and I really liked that option. I kept track (as I always do) and found that I was winning about 50% of the time. While I loved winning more often, I was also a bit frustrated that the computer was able to solve twice as many as me.

Then one day, I accidentally discovered that with this version of the game, the rules had changed so that the games were a lot easier to win. Since that discovery, my winning percentage is around 99%. Immediately after I realized the rules had changed, I won 100 times in a row.

And it seemed like the Universe was sending me a simple message: change the rules and change the results.

So I am creating new rules for my business, for my diet, and for my relationships. I know that I can, because I am in charge.

And I know the results will be better.

What rules are you playing by? Would your results be a lot better if you changed the rules?

Suggested Exercise: Pretend you are in charge, and make up some new rules. See how much your life is improved!

Necessary and Sufficient

I talk to a lot of people who communicate with the Angels.

> Some see them and talk to them all of the time.

> Some just see them or hear them occasionally in their dreams.

And I used to feel a little unworthy because I was not seeing and hearing them, too.

Lord knows I have called out to them thousands and thousands of times,

> But so far, they haven't shown up in a visible and audible way.

But while I was waiting for them to show, I kept busy Awakening thousands and thousands of times, apparently on my own.

Learning to Live a life of incredible Wisdom, Bliss, and Love,

> without hearing a word

> or seeing a single Spirit.

Today I realized that some of the Angel Seers and Communicators I know live a life of great Bliss, Ease, and Comfort, and some live a life of great stress and anxiety.

For the stressful folks, seeing and speaking with Angels has not brought them to a place of permanent or even frequent Joy and Peace of Mind. Some of them seem downright tortured by the experience.

So I realized that I was not limited in any way!

I don't need to see and speak with Angels to become The Angel Within

> I am worthy and capable of connecting with Spirit just the way I am.

And that was my lesson: communication with the Angels is not necessary and not sufficient.

Do you see and hear Angels? Do you know anyone who does? Do you feel like your life is limited in any way without the experience?

Suggested Exercise: Embrace the concept that You Don't Need Anything to connect with Source and become The Angel Within. You can do it right now, with or without the Angels or anything else.

Six Foundational Paths

It has been slowly occurring to me that even though there are hundreds of Paths to Spirit I have discovered and written about, there are some foundational paths that I have yet to describe: Sharing, Understanding, Planning, Giving, Receiving, and Action.

The Path of Sharing happens when I tell my story to others and I am heard. They don't have to give advice, although they often do. Just being heard, being cared about is enough to ease my stress and tension. I know that I am not alone, and I feel safer.

The Path of Understanding happens when I figure something out. Just knowing why I am afraid, or discovering a mistake I have made, or resolving a conflict between opposing ideas helps me feel stronger. "Oh, that's the reason!" is one of my favorite expressions.

The Path of Planning happens when I create a plan of action. When I look at all of the possible things I could do and decide which ones to do first, and then which ones to do next, I feel safer in having made the choice.

The Path of Giving happens when I donate time or treasure to others without any expectation of return. It helps me focus on my blessings and eases my addiction to my possessions.

The Path of Receiving happens when others give their ideas, time, or treasure to me. It helps me feel supported and safe. Their ideas help me Understand and Plan.

The Path of Action happens when I simply do something, anything, to move towards a goal or away from a situation or condition that is uncomfortable. Taking action gets the energy moving in the right direction, opens up channels of inspiration that would otherwise be unavailable, and reduces my stress.

Even though these paths are foundational, they can be incredibly powerful. When my tension and stress is relieved, it often triggers an outpouring of not just Peace, but Joy and Strength, too!

> *How often do you experience on these Foundational Paths? How often do you Give and Receive? Do you feel good when you figure something out or create a plan, too?*
>
> *Suggested Exercise: Practice these paths today. Share with someone, and allow them to Share with you. Be both a good Giver and a Receiver, and see how that feels.*

The Baseline

In my men's group last night, one of my friends talked about his baseline anxiety, in the sense that he is normally somewhat tense and stressed. I think it is a condition that we all share. I think there are very few people who experience no tension or stress whatsoever.

Even though I have been working on myself for 45 years, I still experience a little baseline stress. It is very subtle, but it is there much of the time. Some days, the baseline anxiety is stronger than other days. Sometimes, it appears to have vanished completely.

I think there are many baselines, or "normal" experiences: anxiety, Joy, Peace, Strength, etc. The objective of my Spiritual Journey has always been to lower the negative / shadow baselines while raising the positive / Spiritual baselines.

Over time, what is seen as normal has changed a lot. My level in my Ocean of Love is rising, while the level of my cesspool of fear is decreasing, every day.

So I'll keep Meditating, Elevating, and Awakening every day, until Bliss, Consciousness, and Connection with Spirit are the new Baselines.

What is your baseline anxiety? How do you think it compares with others in your life? How have you changed in the last year?

Suggested Exercise: Think about the people and situations around you and how they impact your baseline levels, both positively and negatively.

Moments

I counted up the Moments in my life today, and there were a lot of them.

First, I defined how long a Moment was, and I settled on three seconds.

> It could have been longer or shorter, but I chose three.

As of today, I have been alive 22,115 days.

And if every Moment is three seconds,

> I have experienced 636,912,000 Moments
>
>> Give or take a few.

Some of them have been in the pit of darkness.

Some of them have been in Union with the Divine.

Some of them have been unconscious.

More and more of them these days are Clear and Awakened.

Seeing this Moment in the context of so many other Moments is quite Humbling.

Six Hundred Million Moments.

One Moment at a time.

Wow.

How many moments have you experienced? Do you see this moment in the context of your lifetime?

Suggested Exercise: Meditate on the next few moments. Step back and see them in the context of your lifetime.

The Depths of My Conditioning

I have been spending a lot of time in Silence or near-silence these days, just watching and experiencing energy shifts at increasingly subtle levels. And I Amazed and Humbled by the Depths of My Conditioning.

As with Pavlov's dog, external and internal events trigger responses at the subconscious levels. The Zings and Buzzes are automatic. Some are large and some are small – they come in a lot of flavors and sizes.

I see an attractive woman and I smile. I see a powerful and serious man and I tense up a bit. I see someone being pompous and arrogant and I prepare for battle. I see others being serious and I become serious, too, and so on.

Then I release my fear by finding a balancing positive energy. I whisper words like Patience, Kindness, Humility, Gratitude, Faith, Confidence, or Sunshine! to myself and the negative energy is washed away.

In an instant, I am healed.

And over time, the Buzzes are getting quieter and less frequent. My Practice of Awakening is transforming me moment by moment.

Soon, I suspect the Buzzes will all be managed quickly, automatically, and subconsciously. Someday, perhaps, I won't even notice them anymore or they will just stop entirely.

And the Zings? Well, when a pretty woman walks by, I just smile. ☺

> *Are you aware of your Buzzes and Zings, or are you still silently screaming at yourself?*
>
> *Suggested Exercise: Become silent. Get in touch with your body. Discover the Depths of Your Conditioning.*

The Cake is Done

I went to a conference last week and found myself telling a lot of people that The Cake is Done.

Sometimes, when we have some resistance, hesitation, or outright fear about doing something, the most helpful thing to do is to take a courageous action. Jump off of the diving board, climb the wall, walk across the fire pit, just do the thing that you are most afraid to do. Then you no longer need fear it.

But sometimes the right thing to do is to continue rehearsing before you sing the song – especially if you are continuing to make progress and especially if it means everything to you.

And it is a great challenge and paradox to choose which strategy to employ: to pull up your shorts, suck it up, and get out on stage, or to wait for a while longer until the timing is just right.

In my case, I have waited for years to come to the point that I am totally comfortable with my Path and my Message.

Now, I am ready to Sing my Songs, Read my Poems, Step Out on Stage, and Share my Experiences – all with great Humility and Confidence.

I have reached the tipping point.

The fear is gone.

The Cake is Done.

What are you working on? Is it time to step out on stage, or could you use a little more preparation? Have you been waiting too long in hopes of perfection?

Suggested Exercise: Think of something you have wanted to do or become for a long time. Ask yourself honestly — are you procrastinating out of fear, or are you intelligently waiting for the right time?

The ABC's of Enlightenment

Amazing – this life is so Amazing

Beautiful – there is Incredible Beauty all around me

Consciousness – I am so Blessed by my Higher Consciousness

Dream – life is but a Dream, and I am the Dreamer

Eager – I am so Eager for the Joy and Love and Blessings that are coming my way

Family – I am Blessed with Family wherever I go

Gratitude – I am Grateful for this Experience of Life

Humility – I am Humbled by the Glory of this Life Experience

Integrity – I maintain Integrity with myself and in all my relationships

Joy – I am Overwhelmed with Incredible Joy

Kindness – I choose to be Kind to Everyone All of the Time

Love – I am Consumed by Love

Moment – In this Moment, right now, I Choose the be one with Spirit

Nature – I love Nature in all of its Magnificence

Open – I am Open to greater Learning and Love

Powerful – I am Powerful beyond measure and beyond my own knowingness

Quick – This life is passing Quickly before my eyes

Ready – I am Ready to Receive

Spirit – I am Devoted to my Divine Essence

Thrive – I am Thriving right now as Spiritual Energy flows through me

Union – I am focused on a complete Union with Spirit

Vibrant – the Light of Love shines brightly onto me, into me, and through me

Wisdom – I grow in Wisdom every day

X-Ray – I see through this moment into my soul and the souls of others

Yes – I say Yes to Spirit and to Love in all of its forms

Zest – I have a great Zest for Life!

What are your favorite words? Do you see how just allowing yourself to be moved by the energy of words can trigger an Awakening?

Suggested Exercise: Repeat this list several times, and then make up your own.

No

I hear a lot of Spiritual Teachers and Coaches saying that it is impossible to focus on the things we don't want without attracting more of it into our lives.

While this makes perfect sense in most circumstances, I find that it isn't always true with me.

My subconscious mind understands the word "no".

For example, when I say "no fear" to myself, it really works to erase my fear. And in my experience, it often works better than words like "courage" or "confidence" or "be brave".

That is because the energy, the vibration of the words "no fear" are very powerful with me. It means there is no fear. With words like "confidence", "bravery", or "courage" carry a little energy of fear and overcoming it.

Maybe it's my math background, but the vibration is clear to me: "no" means "zero", "none", "nil", "the empty set" and it is one of the most powerful vibrations I have.

Or maybe it is that my mother said "no" quite a bit when I was young. ☺

In either case, I get it.

Does "no" work for you? Is it as powerful for you as it is for me? Does it work as well as using a word with an opposite meaning?

Suggested Exercise: Sit in silence and then explore the energy, the vibrations in using the word "no".

Surrender

I Surrender to Spirit, I Surrender to Love
In All Ways, In All Ways,
I Surrender to Spirit, I Surrender to Love
In All Ways, In All Ways,
I Surrender to Spirit, I Surrender to Love
In All Ways, In All Ways,
Now. Now. Now. Now.

And perhaps someday, Always.

When I am Sitting in Silence, it is an Opportunity to Surrender and Love.

When the phone rings, it is an Opportunity to Surrender and Love.

When I am reading emails, it is an Opportunity to Surrender and Love.

When I am doing work of any kind, it is an Opportunity to Surrender and Love.

Everything that happens triggers my Bliss
    When I take the Opportunity
        to Surrender and Love.

When is it easiest for you to Surrender to Love? How many times a day do you do that?

Suggested Exercise: Surrender and Love right now. Make a commitment to Surrender and Love several times today.

Watching From the Stillness

In this next stage of development, I am focusing on Watching All of the Time. I choose to Observe in Silence and Bliss while I am doing, thinking, and feeling, and not succumb to the gremlins and habits of lower consciousness.

Here is a little mantra to help me do so:

> *I am Watching from the Stillness,*
> *Watching from my Bliss.*
> *Not attached to anything*
> *Even thoughts like this.*
>
> *I am Watching from the Stillness*
> *Watching from my Bliss.*
> *Letting go of Everything*
> *Especially poems like this.*

And after repeating this a couple of times, I choose to be Silent and in the Stillness for an equal amount of time.

I know that it is necessary to let go of all my thoughts, even those that helped me let go of everything else.

And it's working.

> *How often during the day are you in a state of detachment, where you are Watching while living?*
>
> *Suggested Exercise:* Practice detachment and Watching today as much as you can. Spend many minutes in the Stillness.

It Takes a Lot of Strength

It takes a lot of Strength to be Humble.

It takes a lot of Strength to be Silent.

It takes a lot of Strength to be Authentic and Open and Honest.

It takes a lot of Strength to Forgive yourself and others all of the time.

It takes a lot of Strength to Surrender to Love.

> *How strong are you? Are you strong enough to be Humble? Are you strong enough to Surrender to Love?*
>
> *Suggested Exercise: Meditate on the strength that is within. Be Humble. Be Silent. Surrender to Love.*

The Wisdom Factory

I have written before about the Bliss Factory and the crap factory: some of the events of life and the thoughts I have are fuel for my Bliss Factory, in that they trigger an outpouring of Joy, Peace, and Love, and other things are fuel for the crap factory, in that they trigger an experience of fear or despair.

In the last couple of days, I became aware of another "factory" of sorts in my subconscious mind: The Wisdom Factory.

Now, all of the output of the crap factory, every little buzz or energy misalignment, every side trip to the shadows, is becoming fuel for my Wisdom Factory.

With each little experience of negative energy, I am reminded to be Humble. I am reminded to Forgive and Love myself, I am reminded of the Amazing Beauty of Life.

Being Humble, Loving, and Wise is a different energy than being Blissful. It is more Peaceful, more Silent, more Serene.

And I am tearfully grateful for the experience.

How big and active is your Wisdom Factory? Do to fuel it with the negative energy you experience so that you can learn from it?

Suggested Exercise: Imagine three factories in your soul: the crap factory, the Bliss Factory, and the Wisdom Factory. Sense which of your life experiences fuel the factories and what their output is.

Morning Prayer

It is a new day and I choose to live this day Aligned with Spirit.

I choose to live this day Awakened and Aware.

I choose to live this day Joyous and Free.

I choose to live this day Present and Powerful.

I choose to live this day Peaceful and Patient.

I choose to live this day Conscious and Clear.

I choose to live this day Constantly Shifting my Energy towards the Divine.

I choose to live this day Consumed by Love.

(repeat many times)

What choices are you making for today?

Suggested Exercise: Create your own Morning Prayer and repeat it for the next several days.

Life is a Celebration!

I Celebrate this Amazing Life!
I Celebrate this Amazing Moment!

I Celebrate the Differences between you and me.
I Celebrate your strong Opinions and your Assertiveness.
I Celebrate your Passion and your Enthusiasm.
I Celebrate your Intensity and Determination.
I Celebrate your Warrior Energy.

I Celebrate my Independence.
I Celebrate my Patience and my Confidence.
I Celebrate my Openness and my Humility.
I Celebrate my Peacefulness and Silence.
I Celebrate my Joy and Freedom.

I Celebrate my Love.

What are you Celebrating today? Can you Celebrate the differences between yourself and others?

Suggested Exercise: Practice Celebrating today! Make a list of the reasons you have to Celebrate and Party On!

Some Will Think II

Some will think I'm crazy,
Some will find me Wise.
Some will fall in Love with me,
And others will despise.

Some will Love my songs and poems,
Some will turn away.
Some will find The Angel Within,
Others, not today.

But I choose to speak with Courage and Love
My Truth to share so sweetly.
So I may serve the ones I can,
While Loving All Completely.

Which will you do? Are you inclined to listen to more of my poems and songs, or are you turning away?

Suggested Exercise: Step out in Courage and Love to share your truth today. Let the others think what they will.

The Lineup

I developed a new and challenging exercise today that is working really well.

I think about all of the people that I really Love and would Love to be with: my Family, some great Spiritual Teachers, famous celebrities, and other really cool people. It is so easy to Love them! I imagine them all standing together on the right side of the room, eager for me to join them in a Celebration!

And then I think about all of the people that I would not like to spend time with. People with whom I have had some issues over time. People who made me angry or wronged me in some way. People whose arrogance or other negative energy is frightening to me. I imagine them all standing together on the left side of the room, waiting for me to come over to them so they can attack and abuse me.

And I ask myself the critical question: do I love the ones in the second lineup as much as the ones in the first? Would I support them and help them as much? Do I remember that they are only trying to protect themselves and rescue themselves from their own darkness? Am I taking their actions and attitudes personally?

And the answer is almost always "no", and I know there is some growing to do.

So I do it. I imagine myself walking over to the ones on the left, and taking them by the hand, one by one, to the other side of the room. There, in the presence of those I Love, I Embrace them and they become one of The Loved Ones.

And in that way, I come to that place where I Love Everyone the Same.

And it is then and only then that I can Love Myself Completely.

> *Are there people in your life in both groups? How many are there in each group? Why are you placing each person in one group or the other?*
>
> *Suggested Exercise: Create your own lineup. Practice taking the ones in the not-loved group to the Loved group. And don't forget to take yourself.*

Something in Store

I had this deep sense today that God / Universe / Source had something in store for me. That all of my work so far, this incredible Inner Journey, this Discovering, Remembering, Embracing, and Becoming my Higher Self day after day after day for so many years, would have a Purpose.

I have never felt like I had a Purpose or a Calling before.

That must sound a little unusual, as so many other Spiritual Teachers / Coaches / Mentors express their own Calling or Purpose, but my truth is that I have never had one.

I've wanted one many times, of course, because feeling that there is a Right Path and Knowing that I am on it would be a tremendous source Safety and Security. For many people, it reduces or eliminates a deep fear of screwing up their entire life.

But I know that I don't need a Calling or Purpose to feel perfectly Safe and Secure. I am very much OK with just Experiencing Life. If I passed away today, I would have nothing but Love for myself. I would never condemn or reject myself in any way. I have tried my best, worked hard, Loved and Lived with great Enthusiasm, and I have no regrets.

But still, there may be a Calling or a Divine Purpose, and I am open to that perspective.

God / Source / Universe may indeed have Something in Store for me.

I'm Listening, but I'm not Waiting or regretting.

Have you found your life's purpose or calling? Do you feel like you need one? Are you doing anything to help discover it?

Suggested Exercise: Talk to people about their purpose or calling. Brainstorm possibilities.

The Choice II

And so, here I am.

Sitting here in the Stillness and Bliss
> with the Understanding and the Knowingness
>> that I can Choose to Be and Do
>>> Whatever I Want.

Wondering What I Want.
Pondering.
Waiting…

Choosing.

And here is My Chosen Purpose:
> To help as many people as I can experience more Spirit in their lives.

It's not a Calling or a Destiny.

It's a Choice.

Do you have a Purpose in Life? Is it a Chosen Purpose or an Assigned Purpose? How did you come to know it was your Purpose?

Suggested Exercise: Ask the people you know if they have a Purpose in Life, and whether it is Assigned or Chosen.

After

So what comes next?

What comes after the Great Awakening,
> After Becoming The Angel Within so often
>> That I am The Angel Within almost all of the time?

Respecting.

Accepting.

Forgiving.

Sharing.

Supporting.

Teaching.

Encouraging.

Empowering.

Inspiring.

Guiding.

Nurturing.

Loving.

Being.

Completely,
> Totally,
>> All of the time.

Have you thought about the After? What will you do when you Become Spirit almost all of the time?

Suggested Exercise: Make a list of the things you will do when you Become Spirit, and then do them now.

The Most Beautiful Things

The Most Beautiful Things in Life to me now are:
- Hugs
- Smiles
- Love
- Healing
- Stillness
- Joy
- Health
- Strength and Vitality
- Clarity
- Amazement
- Excitement
- Safety
- Nourishment
- Sleep
- Awakening
- Consciousness
- and Helping others experience any of the above.

What are the Most Beautiful Things in your life? How often are you experiencing them?

Suggested Exercise: Make a list and focus on experiencing more of them more often, every day.

Instead

I am tempted to be a little anxious,

> but I choose to be Calm and Patient instead.

I am tempted to be a little lazy,

> but I choose to be Focused and Productive instead.

I am tempted to be a little worried, concerned, or fearful,

> but I choose to be Lighthearted and Trusting instead.

I am tempted to feel somewhat diminished when I am around powerful and successful people,

> especially if they are arrogant and assertive,
>
> but I choose to be Loving and Wise instead.

I am tempted to be distracted and forgetful,

> but I choose to remember My Chosen Purpose
>
> and help as many people as I can experience more Spirit in their lives, instead.

I could spend a little time in the shadows for so many different reasons,

> but I choose to be Blissful and In the Spirit instead.

What are you tempted to be? Are you giving into those temptations, or are you choosing to rise above them?

Suggested Exercise: The next time you are tempted to be a little upset, bitter, angry, worried, or tacky, choose to be In the Spirit instead.

Overconfidence

I have discovered a new Gremlin to add to my list.

The first five were Fear, Forgetfulness, Complacency, Unconsciousness, and Attachment.

Number six was Unworthiness.

The seventh is Overconfidence:

> the Choice and Willingness to slip back into lower consciousness through a lack of Diligence, Focus, and Humility.

When I am at my best, I focus on Spirit with every breath and every heartbeat. Every thought is from Spirit and for Spirit.

But to maintain that focus requires Humility, Diligence, and Focus.

When I am overconfident, I lose the connection very quickly. I slip back into the habits of lower consciousness and allow myself to be distracted.

> Perhaps I feel strong and believe I will remain strong.

> Perhaps I am just addicted to excitement and my own ego more that I know.

> Perhaps I am incredibly attached to my thoughts, feelings, and experiences.

Hmmm....

Humility.

Diligence.

Focus.

Every step of the journey is just so fascinating!

Are you overconfident? Do you make mistakes or slip back into lower consciousness as a result of a lack of Diligence and Focus?

Suggested Exercise: Practice focusing on Spirit more often today. When you sense that you have slipped a bit, come back quickly. Be Diligent, Focused, and Humble.

Nature Therapy

I worked on my landscaping yesterday for a few hours. It was hot and dirty work. I trimmed the bushes and cleaned up the mess. I filled five large garbage bags with the trimmings. And the patio looks so much better!

While I was working, I sang my songs loud enough for the neighbors to enjoy. I don't know if they did, but they certainly could have.

I Embraced the Stillness.

I was Patient and Focused.

     Never in a hurry.

         In the Flow.

So the Work was not Work at all – it was a Meditation, a Prayer, a Blissful Celebration of Life.

And I am eager to do it again.

When was the last time you really enjoyed working in Nature? What can you do to turn your work into a Meditation, into a Blissful Celebration of Life?

Suggested Exercise: Next time you have any work to do outside, make it a Meditative Experience. Take the opportunity to Remember and Return to Spirit. Maybe you could even sing a little!

The Problem is Not the Problem

I think the tendency of many people, and certainly it was mine for the longest time, is to see problems as "out there".

Someone said a hurtful thing, someone screwed up or failed to take action, things didn't go according to plan, and so on.

I am finding it quite useful to think about every problem or challenge as both a "Head Problem" (not knowing what to do or how to do it) and a "Heart Problem" (where my fear / anger / shame was triggered in some way).

Most often I find that if my fear is not triggered, then problems are intriguing and even fun! I am able to examine with a light heart and a lot of enthusiasm, because I love working puzzles and being clever.

If my fear is triggered in some way, if I am really tagged, then the problem isn't the problem – it is the trigger that unleashes a fearful response learned in my childhood.

Every time.

And solving the external problem, removing the trigger, won't cure the disease. The response will still be there whenever the next stimulus occurs.

So I choose to work on the real problem – my subconscious condition – by examining my emotional responses, discovering the root causes, letting go of old programming, and Returning to Love.

Do you see your problems as being "out there"? Are they all someone else's fault? Do you see the difference between a fun "head problem" and a painful "heart problem"?

Suggested Exercise: Analyze the problems you encounter today. Note which ones trigger your stress in some way and which ones are fun or interesting.

Watching, Watching

Watching, Watching,
Patiently Watching.

Watching, Watching,
Peacefully Watching.

Watching, Watching,
Cheerfully Watching.

Watching, Watching,
Lovingly Watching.

Watching, Watching,
Humbly Watching.

Watching, Watching,
Silently Watching.

Every thought, every feeling, and every action
      Is an opportunity to become attached
      and focus on that experience
           to the exclusion of all else.
And then I Awaken and Return.

Watching, Watching,
Patiently Watching.

Watching, Watching,
Peacefully Watching.

Watching, Watching,
Cheerfully Watching.

Watching, Watching,
Lovingly Watching.

Watching, Watching,
Humbly Watching.

Watching, Watching,
Silently Watching.

Are you Watching or are you attached to your thoughts, feelings, and actions? Are you Watching right now?

Suggested Exercise: Practice being detached today. Practice Watching – Patiently, Peacefully, Cheerfully, Lovingly, Humbly, Silently Watching. All day.

Outer and Inner

My outer may be anxious and stressed
> My Inner is always Peaceful.

My outer may be frightened
> My Inner is always Poised and Confident.

My outer may be hungry or thirsty
> My inner is always Complete.

My outer may feel abandoned and alone
> My Inner is always in Union with Spirit.

My outer may strain for the answers
> My Inner always Knows.

My outer may be attached to my thoughts and feelings
> My Inner is always Detached and Silent.

My outer may be experiencing scarcity and lack
> My Inner is always Embraced by Abundance.

My outer may be confused or unconscious
> My Inner is always Clear and Awakened.

My outer may be serious or grumpy
> My Inner is always Lighthearted and Cheerful.

My outer may be temperamental
> My Inner is always Calm and Steady.

My outer may be judgmental

>My Inner is always Understanding and Kind.

My outer may be troubled by the words and actions of others

>My Inner is always Consumed by Love.

Do you have awareness of your Inner? Are you being your Inner or you outer right now?

Suggested Exercise: Whenever you feel the slightest buzz, focus on your Inner. Make it your practice today.

Ethereal

I talked to a new friend a couple of days ago, and something she said stuck with me.

We were talking about dealing with challenges being sent my way, and I mentioned having my shields up.

She said she had learned to think of being Transparent, instead. I really liked that.

I have been thinking about the concept off and on for a couple of days, and have been taking it further.

So now I am focusing on being Emotionally Ethereal, like a whisper or a ghostly vision. My Ego is not there.

Every bit of negative energy that comes my way

    just flows through me.

There is no resistance or defensiveness necessary,

    because there is no possibility of being harmed in any way.

And I am at Peace.

Do you often find yourself being defensive or resistant? Do you have your shields up? Have you drawn your sword, too, and are you fighting back?

Suggested Exercise: The next time you feel like fighting, try being Transparent or Ethereal, instead.

The Many Ways

There is a dimension of openness when it comes to people who believe in their path. They may believe their religion / path to be:

- The Only way
- The Best way
- My way
- A way
- No way

For those who say "Mine is the Only way",

    I say "No way";

    it is certainly not the "Best way",

        and because of the condemning and rejecting nature of it,

            it may not even be "A way".

But of course,

    That is just "My Way".

Are you attached to your way? Do you understand that there may be many other ways, too?

Suggested Exercise: The next time you find yourself defending your faith, your ideas, or your path, consider that there are many lessons to learn, and there may be many paths to Source.

Easy

I worked on closing the books a couple of days ago, a project I have done more than a hundred times, and found everything quite Easy.

It usually isn't. I usually get just a little stressed about the seven hours worth of tasks.

But this time,

>Completing the expense report was Easy

>Entering all the checks was Easy

>Balancing the checkbook was Easy

>Sending out invoices was Easy

>Reviewing the financial reports was Easy

>>It was All Easy.

It was Easy

>Because I Took It Easy.

By Taking It Easy

>I was Making It Easy.

I Chose to Take it Easy and Make it Easy.

It was Easy!

Are you struggling more than you need to? Are you subconsciously choosing stress over easiness?

Suggested Exercise: The next time you begin to stress about something, think about how easy it could really be. Take it Easy. Make it Easy.

The Journey

The Journey continues, day after day.

Every day I spend some time In the Spirit

        And over time

                More and more time

                    There.

And every day I take steps forward and steps backwards. I stretch towards Source

        and then I get distracted again.

Whenever I think about Source again,

        I come back to The Spirit and move forward.

You may be further along than me right now.

You may be closer to Source.

You may be Stronger, Wiser, more Loving and Joyful, and more Peaceful than I am right now.

        If so, please support me on My Journey.

            And I shall do the same for you.

For the only thing that matters

        is Progress

            on The Journey.

Is your Journey one of taking three steps forward and two steps back, over and over again, like mine?

Suggested Exercise: Practice being of service and being supportive of those who are having a challenging moment on their Journey. The time will come when someone will reach down and lift you up in return.

Today's Focus

Today, I am going to focus on:

    Healing Peace,

    Energizing Joy,

    Transforming Power,

    Guiding Wisdom, and

    All-Consuming Love.

That's it.

All day.

Simple.

Easy.

Effective.

What is your focus today? Is it Simple? Is it Easy? Is it Effective?

Suggested Exercise: Try a simple affirmation or focusing mantra today. Say it to yourself thousands of times.

Before

I have been privileged to be a guest speaker on a couple of radio shows over the last few weeks, and developed the habit of Returning to Spirit before the show began.

I wanted to make sure that Every Word
    and Every Thought
        was coming from My Higher Self;
    that I was "Tapped In"
        and Speaking from Spirit.

I wanted my words to be as Kind and Loving and Wise as they could possibly be,

    because I considered the opportunity
    to Speak about Spirit

        to be a Sacred Opportunity.

And it occurred to me today to Return
before *every* call or meeting or task,

    to make sure that I am coming from Spirit,

        and that my words and ideas are as Kind and Loving and Wise as they can possibly be.

Because *every* conversation is an opportunity
to Speak from Spirit

    And *every* action and interaction can be Sacred.

It's working well.

And I am Deeply Humbled
    that I didn't think of doing it
        Before.

> *When do you make a point to be at your best? Before a job interview or a date? Before an important meeting?*
>
> *Suggested Exercise: Practice Shifting your Energy and Becoming your Higher Self before every meeting, call, or task.*

Yes

I had the most beautiful meditation this morning,

> as I took another step towards Becoming the Angel Within
> more Deeply and more Permanently.

I woke up at 2:30 AM, as I often do, and immediately began my Return to Spirit.

I repeated "Yes, Come, Be, I Am"

> over and over again,
>> for hours.

And I Imagined / Dreamed / Saw myself surrounded by other Angels and Spirits who were my friends and colleagues from another place, but were much more than that – they were a part of me, too.

It was the same Vision I saw some time ago where I Knew that I was a collection of Spirits (much like Abraham) who used to believe that they were individuals in this physical dimension.

And I was Connected, Protected, Guided, and Loved as much as I have ever been,

> perhaps even more so than ever.

It was Beautiful.

Simply Stunningly Beautiful.

When was your last powerful Vision or Meditation? What did you see and experience?

Suggested Exercise: In your next deep meditation, focus on seeing yourself as a collection of spirits in another dimension, living an illusion of separateness and mortality in this dimension.

Even Though III

Even Though I'm still a little afraid that people will misunderstand or condemn me,

> I Deeply and Profoundly Accept All of Me.

Even Though I'm still a little afraid that people will misunderstand or condemn me,

> I Deeply and Profoundly Accept Myself Anyway.

Even Though I'm still a little afraid that people will misunderstand or condemn me,

> I Deeply and Profoundly Accept How I Feel.

And the fear continues to fade away.

What are you still afraid of? Do you Deeply and Profoundly accept yourself anyway?

Suggested Exercise: Substitute your own fear for "... that people will misunderstand or condemn me", and use a technique like Emotional Freedom Technique (EFT) tapping to lower your fear.

Always II

First, you hear about it

Then, you imagine it

Next, you experience it

And then you come back again,

> Come back as often as you can
>
> Come back every day
>
> Come back many times a day
>
>> Until you are There
>> almost All of the Time.

Practice.

Practice.

Practice.

Always Practice.

When did you consciously start your Journey to Spirit? How often are you coming back?

Suggested Exercise: Practice Being In the Spirit for the next hour or so. Then do it again.

No Sacrifice

I was reflecting today on Returning to Spirit

    Deeply

    Completely

    Always.

And as I was repeating these words over and over

    Returning

    Becoming

    Being.

After a while,

    While in the Stillness of Bliss,

        I found myself once again thinking about how long it is taking me to transform all of my habits of lower consciousness

            into Habits of Higher Consciousness.

It is Humbling to Understand how much I have resisted

    Letting Go and Becoming

        All of the Time.

And it came to me that

    It is No Sacrifice to Return to Spirit

    It is No Sacrifice to Become an Angel

    It is No Sacrifice to Become Consumed by Love

    It is No Sacrifice to Surrender to Source.

It is a Privilege
    an Honor
        and a Blessing Beyond Measure.
And once again
    I can hardly see through the tears of Joy and Love.

Why are you hesitating? What are you afraid of? What is holding you back?

Suggested Exercise: Practice Awakening. Practice Becoming. One Thousand Times a Day.

Attachments

I have been reflecting on the many attachments in my life:
> attachments to my money and my possessions
> attachments to my career and my hobbies
> attachments to my names and my titles
> attachments to my beliefs and my opinions
> attachments to my thoughts and my feelings
> attachments to my expected outcomes
> attachments to my food and my drink
> attachments to my books and my songs
> attachments to my games and my stories
> attachments to my paths and my practices
> attachments to my body and my life.

These are the things I hold on to,
> Like a teddy bear or a baby's blanket
>> to help me feel safe.

And the more frightened I am,
> The more tightly I cling to them.

Someday, I know,
> I will put them all down.

What are you attached to? What makes you feel safe? What ideas, possessions, and habits are you clinging to?

Suggested Exercise: Let go of something – anything. Then let go of something else. Change. Allow. Transform. Know that you are safe.

Life

From the moment we are born

> We seek comfort and safety and avoidance of pain.

At first, we are totally dependent on others:

> All of our happiness and protection comes from external sources.

Gradually, we learn to get our own food and drink

> To bathe and clothe ourselves
>> and to make our own way in the world.

We learn to fear

> and we become attached to anything that makes us feel safer.

Some are much more frightened than others

> But we all are deeply frightened and wounded at times along the way.

We develop patterns of attitudes and actions to protect ourselves

> Many of which serve us well as children
>> but not as adults.

We cry, we yell, we smile, we cajole, we perform, we whine, we argue, we withdraw, we complain, we criticize, we fight.

We often develop a deep fear of change and the unknown
    And, not believing in ourselves,
        We give away our power to others,
            Constantly seeking their approval and guidance.

We get tagged and tickled by our external and internal worlds
    And spend a lifetime learning to avoid the tags
        And maximize the tickles
            While healing our deepest wounds.

The reward of healing our wounds and freeing ourselves from our fears
    is to free ourselves of attachments
        and to find Peace and Joy in everything we experience.

Such is Life.

What attachments do you have? What are you clinging to in order to feel safer? What deep wounds from your childhood are you still healing?

Suggested Exercise: Make a list of your wounds and attachments. Pick one. Heal Yourself through Understanding, Forgiveness, and Love.

Stronger and Safer

People do all kinds of creative things to help themselves feel Stronger and Safer.

On the positive side, they may:
- Get into better shape
- Get some education
- Get a better job
- Join a community
- Attend a motivational seminar
- Complete something.

On the negative side, they may:
- Put people down (publicly or in private)
- Break a rule or a law to "get away with something"
- Intentionally hurt someone or damage something.

So when you see someone:

> hurting themselves or someone else,
>
> criticizing others,
>
> breaking rules, or
>
> doing damage,
>
>> You can be sure they are just trying to feel Stronger and Safer.

And, each in his own way,

> is crying out for help.

Do you know someone who is trying to feel stronger and safer by doing damage to themselves or others? Is that someone you?

Suggested Exercise: When you see someone engaged in negative behavior, take a minute to understand them and help them feel stronger and safer in a positive way.

Fear Ladder

First comes the fear,

> Then comes the idea that something "out there" or "in here" can make me safer
>
>> Then comes the Attachment to that something.

I think my deepest attachments are those that were formed early in life

> In response to some really scary or painful situation
>
>> Subconsciously.

They became habits of attitude and action

> And then part of my personality.

Discovering them

> Understanding them
>
>> And Changing them when it serves me
>>
>>> Is the work of my lifetime.

Have you discovered your subconscious attachments and the reasons they are there? Are you healing them?

Suggested Exercise: Remember your greatest pain and your response to that pain. See if it has carried over to other areas of your life, and if it serves you there.

Mahara

I don't communicate with God.

> Or Spiritual Guides.
>
> > Or Angels.

I've always wanted to, of course. I have long wanted to have a close personal relationship with my Ethereal Family. I have prayed to them and called out to them thousands and thousands of times, but they have not responded by replying or showing up.

Like so many others,

> I have always wanted to be Connected, Protected, Guided, and Loved.

So I decided to Imagine God.

I decided to create the Energy of God in my mind and put a label on it. I imagined an Ethereal Energy that embodied all of the virtues that I hold most sacred, in an incredible measure.

And soon afterwards, I had the impression, like a daydream, of a middle-aged Indian woman / queen / goddess.

And when I asked for her name, I was told "Mahara".

Mahara is Infinite Love – far greater than any Love I have ever imagined or dreamed of.

Mahara is Infinite Peace – far greater than any Peace I have ever imagined or dreamed of.

Mahara is Infinite Joy – far greater than any Joy I have ever imagined or dreamed of.

Mahara is Infinite Power – far greater than any Power I have ever imagined or dreamed of.

Mahara is Infinite Wisdom – far greater than any Wisdom I have ever imagined or dreamed of.

Mahara is Infinite Goodness.

Mahara is Infinite Divine Energy.

Mahara is Infinite Life.

And I hold that Energy in my mind as best I can
> Whenever I call the name Mahara.

What Energy do you feel when you call the name of your God? What is the Greatest Goodness that you can imagine?

Suggested Exercise: Define all of the attributes you would ascribe to your deity, and then give the collection a name. Create your own God, as I have done.

Maharami

Once I had created Mahara, my personal concept of Infinite Divine Energy,

> I began to hold the thought in my mind
> of becoming One with this Divine Energy,

having it Flow onto me

> into me

> and through me.

Filling me.
Healing me.
Transforming me.
Elevating me.

Until once again,

> I am the best that I have ever been.

Until once again,

> I am The Angel in Me.

I am Mahara and Mahara is me.

> Maharami.

And just like that, there it was –
> the name of The Angel Within:

> Maharami.

> *Have you given a name to The Best You Can Be? What is that name?*
>
> *Suggested Exercise: Describe yourself when you are at your best. Give The Angel Within a name, and call it often.*

About the Author

Paul Hoyt has three great passions in life and has been pursuing excellence in each of them for over 40 years.

First, he is a Business Consultant who is passionate about helping business owners and senior executives develop and execute growth plans, whether they are just getting started in business or preparing to sell. He is an expert at startup sequencing, strategic planning, financial modeling, capital engineering, all kinds of analytical tasks, and "getting the job done". His business books and information products, *The Foundation Factor* (2004), *The Capital Coaching Program* (2010), and *Beyond Business Survival* (2013) have been well received by many.

Second, he is a Speaker and Performer who enjoys opportunities to speak or sing, whether the audience is a single person or thousands. He speaks on a variety of subjects and sings in a variety of styles, with business growth and spirituality being his favorite speaking topics and musical comedy and spiritual lullabies being his favorite performing genres. If you want to see a lot of people smile, simply put him in front of an audience. If you want to be inspired, ask him to sing you a beautiful song.

Third, he is a Spiritual Mentor who loves having meaningful conversations about the nature of reality and the development of consciousness. He studies the masters and does inner work for hours every day. He loves thinking and talking about the meaning of life and human potential. He loves transformational tools that work.

This is his third Inspirational work. He published *Remember - A Simple and Gentle Pathway to Spirit* in 2005, and *The Practice of Awakening – 150 Ways to Raise Your Consciousness Whenever You Choose* in 2010.

(see www.RememberTheSpirit.com and www.ThePracticeOfAwakening.com).

You can learn more about him at www.PaulHoyt.com.

www.ingramcontent.com/pod-product-compliance
Lightning Source LLC
Chambersburg PA
CBHW071650090426
42738CB00009B/1480